"If you want to win, you must stop letting ... ... and start making things happen. Leona shares strategies to make things happen and will help you fill in the gaps that are preventing you from reaching your goals. I highly recommend you read this book and re-read it, and share it with your friends. You will be glad you did!"

Willie Jolley
Award Winning Speaker and Media Personality
and Best Selling Author of "A Setback Is A Setup
For A Comeback" and "Turn Setbacks Into
Greenbacks!"
www.williejolley.com

"HEAR APPLAUSE is so much more than a book. It is a comprehensive navigation system for those determined to reach their own pinnacle of success! Pick it up... but only if you are willing to defy mediocrity and pursue all that is possible for you. Leona's words will challenge you, inspire you and leave you asking, 'WHO AM I TO PLAY SMALL?'"

B. Michelle Pippin
Founder of Women Who Wow
Small business marketing expert
Speaker and author
www.womenwhowow.com

"Leona challenges you to be proactive in your pursuit of personal and professional success. Simply taking one small successful step at a time will yield big results. Then you, too, can say, 'I did it! I hear that applause!'"

Sandra Yancey
Founder & CEO
eWomenNetwork, Inc.
Producer: The Glow Project movie
www.ewomennetwork.com

"Leona has a delightful, gentle way of powerfully changing your perspective."

Kim Duke
"The Sales Diva"
Internationally known speaker, author, and coach
www.salesdivas.com

"Inspirational! This book shows how positive thinking can change your life for the better."

Jean Oursler
J. Alden Consulting Group, Inc.
www.jaldenco.com

HEAR APPLAUSE!

Julie —

I applaud YOU!

Thank you for all you do to encourage & empower others to

Hear Applause!

Leona
5-26-10

HEAR APPLAUSE!

CHOOSING SUCCESS IN 12 STEPS OR LESS

LEONA M. LA PERRIERE

Leona M. LaPerriere

GREENSBORO, NC

Published by Applause Publishers™
PO Box 9396, Greensboro, NC 27429

Visit us online at www.HearApplause.com

ISBN 13: 978-0-9843137-3-0
LCCN: 2010903477

First Applause Publishers™ printing, March 2010

"To dream anything that you want to dream,

that is the beauty of the human mind.

To do anything that you want to do,

that is the strength of the human will.

To trust yourself, to test your limits,

that is the courage to succeed."

Bernard Edmonds

This book is dedicated, in loving memory,
to my mother, Rita Dupont.

Her smile, her positive, can-do attitude, her goodness, and her
energy radiated love to all who came in contact with her.

She made a difference in people's lives. She
was, and still is, an inspiration.

This book is also dedicated to my husband, Dan.

He has no idea how much I value him as my
husband, best friend, and colleague.

He is a treasure beyond compare.

In Appreciation and Thankfulness

I would like to call these wonderful people up on the stage to take a bow and get some well-deserved applause. Anything worth doing is worth doing well, and when one has the support of some incredible people, the goal becomes attainable and enjoyable. But where do I start? Well, perhaps I will give thanks to those who have been my greatest supporters, friends, inspirations, and cheerleaders throughout this endeavor. They are treasured in my personal and professional lives and their input has added much value as we worked through the various stages of this book. They have made me feel that I could actually accomplish this dream. They have my deepest appreciation.

From the very beginning, my husband, Dan, has been there lovingly encouraging me, inspiring me, and keeping me grounded in reality. He is my rock. His wonderful sense of humor has kept me in balance and relieved a lot of the pressure I put myself under. He believes in me and gave me the "space" to develop this dream I had.

My children and their spouses and significant others have borne the brunt of my questions, revisions, and anxieties—I appreciate you, value you, and thank you from the bottom of my heart: Dan and Kate La Perriere, Michelle and Gaby Mahalin, and Monique La Perriere and Kellen Nelson.

I appreciate the quiet support and encouragement of the Lattitude Group. Kathy and Dan graciously gave me the time necessary to work on this project, attend specific conferences and seminars that would be relevant to this book, and reduce the number of new clients that I might have taken on.

"Simply" Sue Falcone has been a cheerleader and brave heart to do the first edit of my book and to be a true friend and confidante as I went through this process. Her own experience as a writer added value to the messages I wanted to impart to my readers.

My sister Estelle Leger also spent countless hours reading through my revisions and adding her thoughts as to what was best for my readers. Thank you for always being there along the way.

Michelle Pippin, (Women Who Wow!), is my coach and is the one who first challenged me to go out of my comfort zone and do something big and bold. Who would have thought this was what I was going to do!

Kristen Eckstein, from Imagine! Studios, has had to put up with all my ideas and revisions. She has done this with professionalism, integrity, and a smile. I am thankful that she has been my partner as she guided me through the writing and publishing process.

I've enjoyed my conference calls with Jan King, Founder and Editorial Director with eWomenPublishingNetwork.com, and I appreciate her valuable insight, expertise, and creative suggestions.

The support team at Resource Associates Corporation always encourages their affiliates and associates to reach for the stars. Their dedication to quality and personal and professional development is second to none.

Don Clark from DLC Media Group has the patience of Job! It has been a pleasure working with him and a positive learning experience, as well, as Don worked with all of us to produce an outstanding audio product.

I'd also like to include my clients who have entrusted me with coaching them and helping them reach new levels of success. It is through their encouragement and their suggesting that I actually write a book, that I gave it some serious thought and pursued the challenge.

So much appreciation goes to all the "guests" in my book who have shared a part of their lives with us. They have added much value and personal experiences to the success steps in this book. I appreciate their trust in our friendship and their willingness to be open for our readers. I am humbled by your generous spirit.

And last, but not least, I thank you, the readers, for believing that you are worth the effort as you continue on your path to personal and professional growth.

Table of Contents

About the Music

You will notice that each chapter is introduced with 2 songs being featured. This is how it came to be:

Music is an international language. I was looking for a commonality that people could relate to. Music speaks to people's souls.

I asked many people to submit a song that they like to listen to or sing to when they are feeling in a funk, needing a little boost in their morale, or just to feel better...something that gets them going.

I asked for the title of the song, the artist, the name of the person submitting the song, where they were from, why they liked and chose this song, what they did, and their business Website or e-mail address.

Then I sorted through all the submissions and selected the ones that I felt most complemented each particular chapter and the processes being discussed in that chapter.

All the submissions are acknowledged and listed at the back of the book. I offer a heartfelt thank you to everyone who helped in this endeavor.

"I'm Alive!" by The Hooters

Submitted by Alan Kovitz, Camden, Delaware

"There are certain songs that bring us back from dark places or boost us from good to great. I start my day with this beauty and instantly energize myself to enjoy the day to its fullest. You can do the same!"

Alan is the CEO of Elevations Unlimited. He is coach to the world's most successful entrepreneurs and entrepreneurial organizations.

Learn more at: www.elevationsunlimited.us and/or alan@elevationsunlimited.us

"Shining Star" by Earth, Wind and Fire

Submitted by Lisa Romano, Egg Harbor, New Jersey

"I submitted this song because, over the years, it has been a mantra to me. It encourages me to appreciate who I am and use my strengths to achieve my goals."

Lisa is a multimedia artist working from her studio—Art & Soul Design Studio.

Learn more at: sandlark1@comcast.net

Dear Reader,

Congratulations! I applaud you for being proactive and giving yourself permission to succeed. In today's competitive world, we are responsible for creating our own opportunities. Yet so many times we set ourselves up for failure; it's in the little things we do, or don't do. It's how we communicate with ourselves. It's how we put things in perspective. Sometimes we have the best intentions, but don't really know how to go about it. How often do we feel that **we** might be part of the problem?

I coach people to success, encouraging them to think with the end in mind. Sounds like it should be easy, doesn't it? However, we are captives of our own conditioning, most of it in a negative form, limiting us in achieving our goals. So how do we transform that negative "stuff" to positive "stuff" and move on to the life we really want for ourselves? How do we transform *instant* gratification to *sustainable* gratification? How do we empower ourselves for success? How do we become part of the solution? How will we hear more applause than boos?

We will do some paradigm shifting while we craft our new potentials and that applause will definitely be forthcoming. Yes, it is more within our control than we realize.

I will share with you some positive thinking and action skills that have had a high success rate with the young professionals and college students that I've coached. For instance, it is quite encouraging for my "collegepreneurs" and young professionals when being able to think "out of the book" becomes the norm. How cool is that! Developing the leadership skills and the soft skills that employers are looking for—such as a positive attitude, effective communication, critical thinking, time management, and financial independence, goal setting and achievement—while in college, really gives my college students and young professionals that all-important edge when applying for internships or jobs. These all-important skills also come in handy when dealing with day-to-day situations and will work for anyone—at any age.

As an entrepreneur, I've used many of these techniques myself when I'm falling into a negative mode and need to prevent a negative spiral. Hey, we're all human!

We will be discovering and developing your "innerpreneur." The *American Heritage Dictionary* defines an *entrepreneur*, which is a word that we tend to be more familiar with, as "a person who organizes, operates and assumes the risk for a business venture."

Using this definition as a base, let us explore what an "innerpreneur" is.

Well, *entrepreneur* is from the French root of *prendre*—to take, and the French word *entreprendre*, which translates to—to undertake. Would you agree with me that an *innerpreneur* is one who undertakes the responsibility to organize, operate, and assume the risk for personal, scholastic, or business ventures, basing the success on the inner strengths and capabilities that one possesses? Wow! That kind of covers a lot of territory!

If you are a successful innerpreneur, would that increase your chances of being a more successful entrepreneur?

Paradigm shift:

Are you still an entrepreneur if you work for someone else? Are you still an entrepreneur if you are part of a business venture? Are you still an entrepreneur if you are in charge of a family or school?

I challenge you to be honest with yourself about what it will take for YOU to be successful. Get down to the nitty-gritty details. Let's fill in the gaps that are hindering your success. Don't skimp on yourself. Be bold. Remember, success is not a coincidence.

My own coach, Michelle Pippin, loves to remind me that my future is created by what I do *today*, not tomorrow. Also, she loves to challenge me to think BIG and BOLD. This goes for you, too. So what are you waiting for? The choices you make today shape your world tomorrow. Not making a choice is still making a choice. So why not choose what you want and need instead of letting life or others choose for you? Your choices *should* be big and bold, and maybe even give you the goosebumps if you truly want to experience success and even reach your dreams. Have faith in yourself and in others around you. Don't underestimate yourself.

Together we will work on some plans that will improve and add positive impact to your professional as well as to your personal life. "Mind the Gap!" is what one hears when getting on The Tube in London. So mind **your** gaps and you will not fall into the cracks or miss the train! As my friend Nancy Perez says, "Success or failure isn't the big things you do right or wrong, it's all the little things you put into action and think about daily."

Taking one small successful step at a time will increase your confidence in yourself and others and also give you permission to be more comfortable with your new levels of success and personal power. After all, even the Lord didn't do it all in one day. What makes us think we can?

What are the gaps that are holding you back from being the very best you can be?

If you are interested in some proven suggestions that will change your way of thinking and lead you to more success, then read on and see how together we can get you hearing more of that applause!

FYI...

Contrary to popular belief, you really do not have to follow chapter by chapter when reading this book. It's perfectly OK to choose the chapters you feel you need the most. Remember that one small change can yield big results! Small changes have a big impact. It's your choice! Go! Enjoy!

Your partner in success,

Leona

"We Weren't Born to Follow" by Bon Jovi

Submitted by Dan La Perriere, Greensboro, North Carolina

"This song brings to mind what type of men my father, Conrad A. La Perriere, and my brother, Conrad L. LaPerriere, were. Both of these men were not afraid to be their own person, to do the right thing at the right time, to overcome obstacles in an honorable fashion, to model leadership values, to initiate change, and to have the courage to follow through. It's been an honor to have had both of these special men in my life."

Dan is CEO and co-founder of The Lattitude Group—a firm specializing in Strategic Business Planning and Leadership/Management Development. Since 2002, The Lattitude Group has delivered results for more than 160 clients in 20+ industries throughout the U.S. and Canada in the for-profit and non-profit sectors.

Learn more at: www.lattitudegroup.com and/or dan@tlgrp.com

"New York, New York" by Frank Sinatra

Submitted by Joan Calvert, Greensboro, North Carolina

"This incredible city vibrates with excitement, opportunity, competition, and vitality. It holds many happy memories for me. One can just feel the pulse and energy of this city. It provides opportunities to succeed no matter who you are; if you can make it here, you can make it anywhere."

Joan is a Community Service Representative with Home Instead Senior Care—the Triad's most trusted source for affordable companionship and non-medical home care for seniors.

Learn more at: www.homeinstead.com and/or jcalvert@homeinstead.com

Introduction

HEAR APPLAUSE!

APPLAUSE!!! Just the thought puts a smile on your face and probably starts a chain reaction in your mind, heart and body. You're probably reliving a wonderful memory or envisioning and anticipating a wild success.

Don't only read the word, but actually say it out loud.

Come on now…**APPLAUSE!!!** Again…**APPLAUSE!!!**

You can have fun with this.

Say it quickly.

Applause!!! Applause!!! Applause!!! Applause!!! Applause!!!!

You've probably added a fist pumping the air as you said it this way. Maybe you automatically started to clap your hands. You probably started laughing!

Now say it slowly.

AAAPPPLLLAAAUUUSSSEEE!!!

Savor the feeling. Does it feel like a warm embrace?

Applause is synonymous with success.

Now pause and think of what applause means to you. When was the last time you heard applause, whether it was for you, your team, or someone else? Was it in appreciation of a job well done? Music well played? A sport well executed? An achievement well earned? Did you feel that sense of accomplishment? Did others share in this applause or was it an internal applause? Does it count if you give yourself applause or does someone else have to applaud you to make it count? When it's only you who hears the applause, is it still applause? It is kind of like the tree that falls in the forest. Does it make noise if no one hears it? No matter. Applause is applause.

There are different kinds of applause, too. Does applause only happen when two hands are clapping together? Can you think of different kinds of applause? How about a "V" for a victory sign, a little wink acknowledging that you witnessed the feat and are happy, a loud "Yahoo!", a little OK sign with your pointer finger circled to and touching the tip of your thumb? How about whistles, a "thumbs" up, or maybe just a secret signal you and another person have for each other? Would you agree all count as applause?

If we look at nature, would you agree that a rainbow is nature's applause after a clearing storm? How about a flower bursting into bloom? One can almost hear the cymbals clashing! How about the caw-caws of a crow after he has just found that ideal corn patch? How about fireworks on the Fourth of July as part of the celebration of the independence of America?

I'd like to get you thinking in different ways about ordinary things so that you will be preparing yourself to do extraordinary things and will hear lots of applause. Perhaps you will realize the importance of helping others hear applause for what they have accomplished. Teach others how to help themselves hear applause. The common term for this is "thinking out of the box," but we will have to come up with some new terms to help us express our new way of thinking as we change our perspective on ourselves. No common, ordinary stuff for us. Why? Don't you want to hear that applause? Applause is for things that are a little bit better, or a lot better, than ordinary. Hearing applause and giving applause, internally or externally, at the end of something attempted, worked on, and achieved is not just a nice option. **I consider it mandatory as a success skill.** Are you up for the challenge? Come join me as we set ourselves up for success and for applause! I want you to enjoy waking up to YOU!

This book is meant to be interactive, so when I encourage you to contact me about your thoughts, suggestions, activities, and results, don't be shy. Share with me, e-mail me, and I'll share with others. Wherever you especially see: *Please share with me...* please do share!

Also...and THIS IS IMPORTANT...I am very interested in hearing your stories about any changes that happened to you in your life as you read and work on the success skills in this book. Did the success skills you chose to apply to your life make any positive changes in your life? How?

I am planning on using these stories in a future book. Please send your stories to:

leona@hearapplause.com

Describe a time when you heard a quiet, internal applause after accomplishing something challenging.

_____

_____

_____

Describe a time when you heard loud, public, external applause after accomplishing something challenging.

_____

_____

_____

Do you feel that a quiet, internal applause is just as satisfying as a loud, public, external applause? Why?

_____

_____

_____

Do you appreciate the applause more if you had to work for it or if it just happened?

_____

_____

_____

How do you feel when you help others hear applause?

_____

_____

_____

"The Man in the Mirror" by Michael Jackson

Submitted by Paul W. Jones, Jr., Detroit, Michigan

"Make changes in yourself first. It's all about being happy and proud of the person you are. This could inspire others to make needed changes as they look to you as a positive example."

Paul is a Success Coach for business professionals and the President and CEO of Plus 3 Solutions, LLC.

Learn more at: plus3@comcast.net

"Feeling Good" by Michael Bublé

Submitted by Kerri Sneed, Pfafftown, North Carolina

"After I suffered a job loss last winter, I challenged myself and started my own business. This song really inspired me on a new path and made me believe I would be successful."

Kerri is the President of Starboard Accounting & Consulting.

Learn more at: www.starboardaccounting.com and/or kerri@starboardaccounting.com

Habits and Hidden Potential

Habits will either make or break us. Habits are not formed in a minute, an hour, or a day. Habits are not formed easily and cannot be broken or changed easily. They are formed over time and by repetitive listening and doing. Habits affect our personality, our attitudes, and our goals. Since a habit is something we do without consciously thinking about it, it takes awareness, commitment, time, and perseverance to form new habits or change or break old habits. Any time you can look yourself in the mirror and say, "Hey, I don't like such and such about me," you have the option, ability, and power to exchange a bad habit for a better one and be more in control of a positive change in your life. If a habit is stopping you from accomplishing something important, it's a habit that needs to be changed. It's not always easy, but it is possible. Habits affect the results we are looking for. Therefore, I challenge you to stretch a little further than you are comfortable with. So often it is our comfort zone that keeps us from making the uncomfortable efforts that are necessary to get us moving and getting things done. It is perfectly acceptable to ask for help or support as we are developing new habits or breaking old habits and stretching just that little bit further.

Rock Climbing

Our adult children and many of their friends are rock climbers. Rock climbers, you say? What on earth does rock climbing have to do with habits and hidden potential or any part of success? Besides the fact that this is a big, bold sport and that it gives me the goosebumps to watch my kids and their friends actually rock climb, let me share the reasons why I chose this particular sport as an example. Climbing demands mental toughness and the willingness to practice hard to master a set of skills. Each climb is a new challenge with new lessons. Climbers need to be focused on maintaining balance and moving forward. Although rock climbing is lots of fun, it is also serious business. The relationship between partners is the most vital component of successful climbing. A climbing partner should be someone that you enjoy spending hours or days with but must also be someone that you can trust and communicate with in very difficult situations. Climbing partners must pay attention to one another at all times, make safe and educated decisions both together and independently, and be able to adapt to changing circumstances. These characteristics become more important as the level of risk increases, perhaps due to weather, exposure, altitude, or to the length or difficulty of the climb. In many cases, there is very little room for error.

As a climbing team, one person acts as the belayer while the other person climbs. Belaying is an important technique climbers must master. The belayer is the climber's safety person who uses various devices and techniques to give or take up slack in the rope and to provide friction on the rope. The belayer assures that if the climber falls, the fall is not far. There is a specific preclimbing ritual followed by climbers worldwide. The climbing team puts on their harnesses, the belayer puts the rope through the belay device, and the climber is tied in. Then the climber says, "On belay." This is a signal for the team to look over each other's harnesses to be sure they are on correctly and to check their knots and belay device to be sure the rope is properly secure. Once this has been done, the belayer says, "Belay on." This signals that the climber can approach the wall and prepare to climb. When the climber is ready to begin, he or she will next say, "Climbing." The response from the belayer, signaling readiness to manage the rope and monitor the climber, is "Climb on." This is a safety ritual or habit that is engrained in all climbers.

Our children and their friends learned the basics of rock climbing at an indoor climbing wall. Outdoors they advanced to top-roping where the rope is already placed through an anchor at the top of the climb. Thus, the rope goes up from the belayer, through the anchor at the top of the climb, and back down to the climber. As the climber ascends, rope is taken up by the belayer. Top-rope climbing offers a rock climbing experience with minimal risks. The rope is always anchored above the climber, so he or she will only fall a few feet and is unlikely to get injured. Top-roping allows athletes the luxury of concentrating on climbing techniques rather than worrying about the dire effects of gravity. Climbers can work on new techniques or just do laps on routes to build strength and endurance. At the same time, the belayer can practice his or her duties, which include checking knots and harnesses for safety, managing the rope with dexterity, and following the rhythm of the climber. The belayer must never take his or her hand off the brake line until the climber is on the ground. This is another important habit that climbers have developed and they know how valuable this habit is.

The partner relationship becomes most important during lead climbing and multi-pitch climbing, where a leader may need to place his or her own protection. The belayer must watch and predict the leader's movements and the team must work together to find the correct route, organize equipment, and move swiftly from a starting point high off the ground.

Basic climbing skills keep climbers safe. Even though these athletes do quite a bit of climbing, they do not take their climbing skills for granted. They never fail to go back to the basics to rehearse their skills and make sure their partners are doing the same. This is an important habit that they have developed and they know how valuable and life-saving this habit is.

As you can see, rock climbers use ropes and the strength of their partnerships to keep safe in tough situations and to protect themselves in case one of them falls. You can also "rope up" in life with family, friends, teachers, counselors, coaches, and ministers, or with other trustworthy partners. These ropes might just end up being lifelines. Be safe rather than sorry. This is simply being smart and responsible. Use all the tools and people necessary to help you develop the good habits you need to be successful.

This rock climbing analogy emphasizes the success skills of communication, trust, developing good and sustainable habits, having compatible and motivational teams, and finding your hidden potential—skills that may allow *you* to climb to great heights.

Habits

Now back to the topic of habits.

Many times the word or thought of a habit has a negative connotation.

"He bites his nails. He needs to break that bad habit."

"Smoking is a bad habit."

"He has the bad habit of watching TV while he's studying."

"She has the bad habit of skipping breakfast."

Have you noticed how the words *bad* and *habit* have been joined together? It sounds like the word *habit* is linked to failure. Very seldom do we hear someone say that a habit is good. Usually the action is mentioned instead of the positive habit.

For instance, "Nikki is now getting better grades this semester." versus "Nikki is getting better grades this semester because she has developed good study habits."

"Look how well John plays basketball. He must practice a lot." versus "Getting to the gym early is a good habit that John has developed, and this gives him more time to practice and become a better player."

We tend to forget that positive results come from developing good habits.

One of the secrets to success is to be as specific as you can about goals. If you choose to focus on the positive action that is needed to develop that good habit, this will probably take a little more practice than you would think. Our brains are simply not trained to think that way. However, the results are quite outstanding. Results happen because you choose to take action. In this case it is positive action. You increase the chances for positive results when you focus on positive action. The fact that you have chosen to be specific links the good habit with good action.

Let me introduce you to Kristen Barbee. Kristen is the Assistant Youth First Coordinator of one of the busiest youth centers in Greensboro. She is also the liaison with the Summit Rotary Club's Student Improvement of the Month nominations and awards. Her enthusiasm, ready smile, and sense of calm make her a great asset to our youth and our city. Kristen will now share with us one habit that she has developed that makes a big difference on how each of her days unfolds:

Kristen Barbee

"A good habit that I have had to develop that is crucial to the success of my position is my commitment to doing things right away. I cannot be a procrastinator! I have been blessed with a can-do, take-charge kind of attitude. This definitely works in my favor. I do not like 'surprises' in the fact that if I am not diligent with my duties, snafus will arise and raise havoc with schedules and budgets. I also feel that I am in a position to be a role model for the youth that come to the center. They need to see that I take great pride in how well I do things, how important it is that I do the right things, that I do them right and on time, in a very professional way, and to the best of my ability.

"I know that the youth and the adults count on me and my team for the success and smooth transition of all the programs at the youth center and with the different outreaches in the city. This habit could be one that could be easily dropped by the wayside, and I do work hard at keeping my focus on making this habit a priority. It is rewarding when people notice that the programs are successful because I'm proud of what I bring to the organizations and that I do take my job seriously and they are experiencing success and 'hearing applause.'"

Thank you, Kristen, for being such a good role model and sharing with us how developing good habits helps you be successful. You deserve a round of applause!

Compliments and Positive Feedback

Habits can be developed by hearing compliments or positive feedback. We all like to hear positive things about ourselves. When we hear positive things over and over it encourages us and gives us permission to continue to develop the habits that will sustain that praise. Even though we might grumble and complain about the extra effort it might take to develop a good habit, we find that we enjoy living up to these expectations. After all, we don't want to disappoint anyone, not even ourselves.

"I appreciate the effort Shelly is making about being on time for work. This shows that she is a responsible person," could be interpreted by Shelly as positive feedback. People are taking notice of her efforts and this encourages her to continue to be on time. It will get her thinking of all the positive actions and results that have happened because she chose to start being on time. Perhaps she'll get a raise in the near future because of this effort!

Dan has made a conscious effort to develop the skills and habit patterns that make him a better listener. When he hears people say they really appreciate how he listens to them and they are now experiencing positive results because of it, his good listening habit is reinforced. Chances are Dan realizes this is a good habit, and he will continue to hone his listening skills. Did this good habit just happen? No. Dan chose to put the effort needed into developing the skills involved in being a good listener so that now listening has become a good habit in his life.

This way of thinking will also allow you to be more focused on the action and not so much on the person when you give someone an affirmation or compliment. People like to be complimented and they especially like the compliment if it targets a specific action. It shows the receiver of the compliment that you have really taken the time to appreciate what he or she did.

What are some positive results you have experienced from creating good habits that have allowed you to be successful at something? Come on…I want at least one! Good for you! Give yourself a pat on the back!

Hidden Potential

Good habits need to be pursued, tested, developed, and made an integral part of your life. You need to keep working at it. Do not think that just changing habits is a quick fix to a festering problem.

Don't ever take a good habit for granted. A habit does not respond well to being thought of as an overnight success. Just because you've succeeded at it once or twice, like any well-oiled machine, you need to keep good habits tuned up. Good habits need maintenance to keep them running smoothly.

Developing good habits is essential in achieving goals and hearing applause. This is a choice, a very important choice. In life you get exactly what you choose, so choose wisely. The process of developing winning habits may lead us to discovering hidden potentials in ourselves and others. However, once you've discovered that hidden potential, it needs to come out of hiding! No excuses! Potential is the capacity for growth and development. If it remains hidden, how will you ever see it or use it to the best of your ability? You need to be proactive and create conditions for new habits. What habits will you create to develop and bring forth your hidden potential? It is up to you.

Perhaps now is the time to make a slight *paradigm shift* here: rather than use the usual expression of "hidden" potential," let's turn the expression into "untapped" potential. Using the word *untapped* encourages me to think in a pro-active way, to start thinking in ways of where and how I'm going to be digging and mining for the gold that is inside of me.

It is always the right time to develop new habits; there is never a wrong time to become a *new and improved* version of you.

Jan Clifford is the executive director of HORSE**POWER**. She is passionate about this program, which offers opportunities to people with disabilities, especially children and youth. Oftentimes they are encouraged to develop new habits that will enhance their quality of life. She believes that these new habits bring out many untapped potentials that her riders and their parents or caregivers were not aware of. She is an inspiration to anyone who comes in contact with her. She is kind, yet firm. Jan, please share with us the "magic" of HORSE**POWER**:

Jan Clifford & Dakota

"I am always happy to have an opportunity to share my passion. We are privileged to interact and work with people who participate in this therapeutic equestrian program that provides both challenges and rewards to people with physical, mental, emotional, and social disabilities. Through interaction with horses and horseback riding, these individuals derive educational, physical, and social benefits that include learning new skills, building self-confidence, enhanced physical fitness, increased muscle strength and flexibility, interpersonal skills, patience, and self-discipline. Very often bad habits must be changed, and new habits developed and put in place. After all, there is comfort in doing things the way you always have done them. You do those things even if they do not offer you the satisfaction you feel you should have, just because they are what you are 'comfortable' with or they are 'what you've always done.' For many, this is not an easy task. They have hurdles to overcome, hurdles that are not your typical, every-day type of hurdles. We're talking about hurdles or disabilities that may include multiple sclerosis, autism, cerebral palsy, spinal cord injuries, Parkinson's disease, Down's syndrome, stroke, and depression, as well as the consequences of physical, mental, or emotional abuse. Yet, these individuals come to see the benefits of forming new habits and discovering so much untapped potential within themselves. Their lives are enriched through this program, thanks to our certified instructors, dedicated volunteers, generous donors, and trained horses. Because the benefits are too numerous to share with you in this limited space, and I really could go on and on about this—why not take a little coffee break and visit our website at www.horsepower.org and enjoy reading the testimonials that are there. Better yet, come on by for a visit!"

Thank you, Jan. I have visited HORSE**POWER** several times and always come away impressed by all the good that is being done there. You and your team most definitely deserve a hearty round of applause—plus!

Routines

We are naturally drawn to repeat what works for us. We make changes accordingly if our lifestyle changes or if we see that something no longer works for us. Our familiar world gives us security—we know what works and what doesn't, what will give us success and what won't. Our daily routines are comfortable. We don't have to think too much about them. However, if you feel that you are in a slump, simply change one thing in a routine and see what happens. You don't have to change your entire life. Maybe it's simply changing the route you take to work, or where you sit at lunch, or where you decide to do your work. Many times, subtle changes in routine allow you to be more alert and you'll discover things that you have been missing. Oftentimes your creativity is stimulated and you come up with fresher and more exciting ideas. Routines are wonderful to have, but shaking them up every now and then can be quite advantageous. Remember that success or failure is found in your daily routines. So make sure your routines are success-bound!

Positive Thinking

One of the most important habits you can develop is **positive thinking.** We need to open our minds and hearts to see how something can be accomplished. In most cases, we have been conditioned to think the opposite. Many times our thoughts and reactions tend to lean on the negative. This negative slant does not have to have the words *NO* or *NOT* in it, but the thought comes out as a negative message.

Here comes a paradigm shift...

For instance, we may hear ourselves saying, "I hate being late."

To hate being late is a good thing. However, it is a negative message and our brain cannot think in a positive way on how to accomplish this. Since the thought was on being late, the brain tends to want to think of ways to be late. You don't want to hear your brain saying, "How can I be late?" After all, that is not what the goal is. What is the goal? The goal is to be on time. If we restate "I hate being late." to "I enjoy being on time." or "I respect other people's time." the brain can now work in a positive way in getting us to think of how many ways we can be on time. These could be to take a different road, get up earlier, have an outfit picked out and ready to go for the next day, or have the lunches made the night before.

Getting the brain to work in a positive way also ignites some positive internal rewards of being a problem solver, being in control, showing responsibility, being confident, and experiencing less stress.

Some positive external rewards could be a smile on your face or a self-confident walk or driving more carefully since you now are not in a rush. **Positive Thinking**.

Another example is: "I hate being fat." Yes, it is a good thing to not want to be fat. What is the goal? Let's turn that around to: "I would enjoy being thinner." "I like having more energy." "I enjoy being healthy." "I love wearing nicer clothes."

Some positive internal rewards to these changes could be more self-confidence, making healthier choices, feeling more empowered, and being proactive.

Some positive external rewards could be having a slimmer body, a bigger smile, a lighter step, and nicer clothes. **Positive thinking.**

OK…One more. How about: "I hate gossiping." What is the goal? Could it be that you enjoy treating people with respect, that you like saying nice things about your friends, and that you want people to say nice things about you? Now your brain can start thinking of ways to do this: hang around with positive people, say kind things to others more often, or change the flow of the conversation to other topics.

Some positive internal rewards could be: having better self-esteem, finding true friendship, not being intimidated by others, and achieving a positive self-image.

Some positive external reactions could be: being able to look others in the eye, staying in a friendship circle with your friends, and confidently smiling more. **Positive thinking.**

If you start to think negatively, such as: I hate being late; I hate being fat; I hate gossiping, and simply go on with your thought process and add… **because**…I enjoy being on time, or I enjoy having more energy, or I enjoy treating people with respect, your brain can certainly work with those positive thoughts better than with the negative ones and will get you to the desired outcomes.

Positive thinking, putting things in positive terms, opens up possibilities and propels you to take action. You become a positive thinker, looking for solutions, being goal oriented.

Is restating your goals a positive step towards finding, working, and developing hidden potential? I say YES!

Should you hear applause when you are making these positive changes and getting the results you are looking for? Absolutely!

List your good habits. How were they developed? Did you need help?

_____

_____

_____

List your bad habits. How were they developed? When do you plan on changing them? Will you need help? If so, who will help you?

_____

_____

_____

Do you think that these habits, good or bad, affect your attitude or self-image? How?

_____

_____

_____

Can you think of ways that you might restate: "I hate being tired" or "I hate getting bad grades" or "I hate getting sick?" Go ahead. Give it a try. You can do it! What would be the internal and external rewards? Remember to be goal oriented—with the end product or vision in mind. If you have other restatements you can share, bring them on!

_____

_____

_____

Please share with me a way in which you chose to change a habit. What were the challenges? What were the results? How did it make you feel? Did you hear applause?

_____

_____

_____

_____

Please share with me if you were able to help someone else change a habit. What were the results? How did this make you feel? Did you and the other person hear applause?

_____

_____

_____

Do you have a routine that is so automatic that you fail even to realize when you are doing it?

_____

_____

_____

One more thought…Watching TV or going to the movies are activities that many people enjoy. But consider what it is you are feeding your brain. Are you feeding your brain high-quality info or junk-food info? Do yourself (and your friends and family members) a favor by interspersing as many movies and TV shows as possible that send positive messages and affirm the qualities we are looking to develop. It'll be refreshing! The more we subject ourselves to affirming media and positive examples and influences, the higher quality life we will experience. We also increase our chances for success. Because we are exposing ourselves to high-quality media, we will be more likely to sharpen our thinking skills and have more power to make better decisions.

"The River" by Garth Brooks

Submitted by Dan La Perriere, Evergreen, Colorado

"This song motivates me to do my best and to face the challenges that come along. One must keep trying to reach his dreams in the best way that he can. There are times one will have to dig deep to overcome obstacles and yet, one must always remember that this must be achieved in an honorable way—with integrity. It is important to never give up. Don't be afraid to be a leader."

Dan is a family practice doctor practicing rural medicine in the eastern part of Colorado.

"This Is My Now" by Jordin Sparks

Submitted by Sydney Collier, Jamestown, North Carolina

"The song talks to me about a time when I hid; I was so afraid, but not anymore. I am now looking ahead. I have uncovered my power and believe in myself. I have so much to give and share and I'm ready."

Sydney is a professional beauty consultant with Mary Kay Cosmetics.

Learn more at: www.marykay.com/s.collier and/or if you'd like, make an appointment with her at: scollier2@triad.rr.com

Ego—Yes! In a Positive Sense

EGO…this word stirs up many feelings, ideas, and psychological mumbo-jumbo. The word *ego*, as taken directly from the Latin, is translated as *I myself*. In modern day society, ego has many meanings. It could mean one's self-esteem, an inflated sense of self-worth, or in philosophical terms, simply one's self. James Harvey Stout, a renowned psychologist, philosopher and theorist, explains ego not only as a complex but understandable piece of our human nature, but something that we can develop and have much control over. For instance:

> "Ego is who we believe ourselves to be. It is our reference point in dealing with the world. Ego is our individuality. It is what sets us apart from others and makes us unique. Ego is our sense of consciousness, an 'eye' from which we look at the world.

> "Ego helps us execute, make decisions, and implement our will. Ego helps us conceptualize, label and organize perceptions, encouraging us to make sense out of the universe and our lives. It helps us as we interface with and try to make sense of the human world of society and individuals. The ego also serves as a mediator as we strive to resolve conflicts involving people and circumstances. It

can also be viewed as a symbol, an achievement of prestige, success, power and pride. Ego can be seen as a pattern, continuity, habits—giving us a sense of security and stability. Another important role of the ego is as a sentry, encouraging us to set personal and societal boundaries."

What does this translate into as we are looking to develop those important skills that will help us effect change in ourselves and others in today's society?

Here comes a paradigm shift...

Ego = pride which produces fear because pride is a negative thing, a "sin"; therefore, punishment will surely follow. Therefore, ego is bad.

This is ego as a negative. We will turn ego into a positive.

Choose to know your strengths and be proud of them. The business and college coaches from The Lattitude Group include as their clients people from many walks of life such as high level executives, large companies, professionals, entrepreneurs, teachers, doctors, students, ministers, parents, and other coaches. Many of them feel overwhelmed and then tend to focus on things that aren't going right rather than to take a few minutes longer to catch their breath and start to think of other possibilities. They neglect or forget to focus on their strengths and fail to use their particular strengths to help them be more successful. They've been conditioned to focus on their weaknesses, or what they do not do well. They've been conditioned to find fault or to blame. Oftentimes our clients begrudgingly tell us about two or three things that they are "OK" at, but we know that there is so much more. Clients tell us they feel they are bragging when they share their talents and strengths with us or with others. Of course, that depends on *how* they share or impart those strengths.

The lesson here is that when you become more comfortable with your strengths, you will see them as an integral part of your being. Sharing your strengths—now, not bragging on them—

then becomes more natural and non-confrontational and more acceptable to all concerned. So take the time to look at yourself from someone else's perspective and imagine what that person might say. It's OK to recognize your talents. Embrace them; develop them; use them; share them. Make a list of your talents and post them in a place that you can easily see as a reminder of how you can make a difference in other people's world, as well as in your own world. The more comfortable you are with yourself and your talents, the easier it will be to develop your innerpreneur. While you're at it, why not make a list of the talents of other people you work with or members in your own family, and post these in a prominent spot? This may encourage you to affirm them, thereby encouraging them and others to live up to their talents. By the way, I am not proposing that you ignore or not do anything about your weaknesses. These do need to be confronted. However, by honing your strengths, your weakness become less and less, and may turn into potential strengths.

This quote from Marianne Williamson's book, *A Return to Love: Reflections on the Principles of a Course in Miracles,* changed my perspective on the meaning of *ego* and gave me permission to go all out in discovering and developing my strengths and talents and sharing them with others:

> "Our deepest fear is not that we are inadequate. Our deepest fear is that we are powerful beyond measure. It is our light, not our darkness that most frightens us. We ask ourselves, who am I to be brilliant, gorgeous, talented, fabulous? Actually, who are you *not* to be? You are a child of God. Your playing small does not serve the world. There is nothing enlightened about shrinking so that other people won't feel insecure around you. We are meant to shine, as children do. We were born to make manifest the glory of God that is within us. It's not just in some of us; it's in everyone. **And as we let our own light shine, we unconsciously give other people permission to do the same.** As we are

liberated from our fear, our presence automatically liberates others."

Bill Mangum, a renowned watercolor artist in my community, is a wonderful example of how using right actions with your talents for the right purposes gives you credibility and can allow for incredible changes in your life and the lives of others.

For the past 21 years, Bill Mangum has created holiday cards for the Greensboro Urban Ministry. Mangum's journey as an artist began with a 59-cent watercolor set he bought while at the University of North Carolina at Greensboro to make his mother a Christmas present, and continues today with a career filled with original works of art and limited edition prints. He admits to once being spoiled by his early success.

Bill will now share with us how meeting a very important person changed his life for the better and turned him into the leader he was meant to be:

Bill Mangum

"A chance meeting in 1988 with a disheveled homeless man helped change my priorities.

The man, Michael Saavedra, was a paranoid schizophrenic. Feeling like a Good Samaritan, I took him to Urban Ministry. On impulse I gave Mike one of my business cards and suggested that he touch base and let me know how he was doing. To my surprise he did just that, and the result was a three-year relationship in which I became his caretaker. It was an amazing contrast to work with someone who had nothing.

"Soon after that, Saavedra began showing up at my church and at my Sunday school class. While some parishioners there embraced Saavedra, others were repulsed. I would even get phone calls, anonymously, from people who said he really can't come to church. And I asked, '*Why* couldn't he come to church?'

"It was uncanny that God was trying to speak to me through all of this.

"Earlier that same year, I offhandedly agreed to paint the cover of the Urban Ministry's new holiday honor card and promptly forgot all about the request. In fact, I didn't think of it again until the neighbor who had approached me asked how it was going. In reality, it should have almost been done. This left me feeling embarrassed and uncomfortable. You see, this nonprofit had begun the fundraiser the year before, in 1987. People who donate at least five dollars got a card to keep or to send to a family or friend informing them a donation has been made in their honor. Hence the name: The Honor Card. It sounded like a good idea at that time, when this friend approached me about painting a card for this cause. It should have been very important to me, yet I *forgot* about it.

"As I searched for inspiration for this card, I found myself one night on South Elm Street at 3:27 a.m. While I was surveying the landscape from the hood of my Jeep, I heard a voice in the distance calling my name — it was Saavedra. The resulting painting, which I titled 'Not Forgotten,' featured a lone man walking with bags in the snow, not far from the old Kress Building, with the flashing 3:27 on the old Jefferson-Pilot clock. We could take it for granted that it's just a beautiful scene. But for me it was life-changing. You see, that card helped raise $53,000 that year for Urban Ministry! To say that was humbling is not even close to how I felt, knowing that I almost hadn't even created that card. Since then, for the past twenty-one years or so, I have been honored to be *the* painter creating the yearly holiday honor card for this Urban Ministry fund-raiser.

"The best part of all this is that also offers so many other people an opportunity to feel they are making a difference in people's lives.

"This mission has also inspired me and my family to volunteer weekly at Urban Ministry. I could easily write a check, but these are real people out there, down on their luck, experiencing losses of some sort, many through no fault of their own. My being with them is inspiring to me. It is a real way that I can give back to community, not just as a 'faceless' painter, but as a real person who really cares. I feel that I've truly got the better end of the deal."

Bill is a true leader. He walks the talk and by doing so, inspires others to do the same. Thank you, Bill for using your talents to make a difference in other people's lives. Thank you for not letting your "ego" get in the way. You definitely deserve a round of applause!

If you'd like to learn more about Bill and what he does, please visit www.williammangum.com and/or www.thehonorcard.org.

To be a leader, having a strong ego is a positive thing. It shows you have a strong sense of self, knowing and working on the person you already are and also the person you aspire to be. Humility comes in as an important factor because it is based on an accurate perception of ourselves and allows us to be unpretentious. When someone says to someone, "Leave your ego at the door," it is to help keep conceit and arrogance under control. A healthy blend of ego and humility gives us an edge for success. Some qualities that help to develop a healthy ego are: independence, self-esteem, personal boundaries, assertiveness, presence, values, freedom, and individuality.

Again, keeping in mind that your ego is really your basic makeup, your real honest-to-goodness self, a God-given gift, would you agree that within you lies your potential for success and happiness? Would you also agree that it is daring yourself to discover and develop your unique talents, dreams and desires?

This is a good time for a little Oscar Wilde humor, "Be yourself; everyone else is already taken."

You have quite a bit of control over your ego; therefore, comparing yourself to someone else when measuring success does not make sense. You don't have to see yourself as less to see others as extraordinary. Learning from the best people in whatever field you are learning about or working in does not mean that you are not smart or less smart than others. Take what you need to help you be the person you envision yourself being. These "extraordinary" people will help you to rise to success and allow you to help others rise to success also. Success may mean something very different to you than it does to someone else. Success is very personal. You certainly may listen to others and learn from them, but be bold and follow your own path. Be careful not to define your personal success by someone else's standards.

Potential

You are gifted with an abundance of untapped potential. As you gain confidence in yourself and in your abilities, you will find yourself setting your sights higher in pursuit of more meaningful goals. Your reserve potential will kick in and you will find yourself more than equal to the task. Do not let your ego fall prey to self doubt, lack of ability, worry about what others will think, fear of failure, or other mental limitations that might keep you from achieving the successes you are striving for.

One would think that the famous and brilliant scientist Albert Einstein would have thought more highly of his "self," his ego, in relation to his potential and all that he added to the scientific world. After all he is known as the "father of contemporary physics," whose work was the foundation for such accomplishments as splitting the atom, discovering black holes, and the Theory of Relativity. However, he wrote that he felt that he used only ten percent of his potential! Perhaps he understood the balance of a healthy ego and humility. How much of your potential are you using or developing each day?

My friend, Lisa Dames, decided that she really did want to pursue a career as a country singer. She was rapidly approaching middle age and did not want to let this dream slip away. Her dilemma: was she being selfish, egotistical, and unfair to her family?

As she worked out all the details on what would need to be done so that all her concerns and priorities were in order, she saw that she could give herself permission to go after her dream. A couple of years ago, as she celebrated her fortieth birthday, one of her songs hit No.39 on the country music chart! She attributes this success to everyone, especially to her family, for working with her in this endeavor. She also takes great pride in being "just" a mother and wife. Let's let Lisa tell us in her own words what that meant:

Lisa Dames

"In 2000 I was sanctioned by the Patsy Cline estate to portray the country music legend in one of two musicals about her life: *Always... Patsy Cline* and *A Closer Walk with Patsy Cline*. After performing in nine productions over a period of five years, I decided that I wanted a chance to perform as Lisa Dames. But it was Patsy Cline's story that gave me the courage to go out and pursue this on my own, with no record label.

"After completing my album, *No One Like Me*, in March of 2006, I loaded up my shrink-wrapped minivan and hit the road for what was supposed to be a ten-day radio-blitz tour. The only other passenger was Sam Frazier, a thirty-year veteran of the Greensboro music scene that I had met through Sound Lab Recording Studios. Ten days turned into a month, and a month turned into two. The tour helped push my first single 'Just Another Day' to No. 56 on the Music Row Breakout Chart, and my second single, 'I'd Leave Me', to No. 39.

"By the time the tour was over, we had spent ten months on the road, traveling to sixty-two radio stations in twenty states. It was during this tour that I came to a few realizations. With a family I deeply missed and a hometown I longed for, I decided that becoming a country music star wasn't necessarily the way for me to go. I had two options: one, to give up and the second to find a Plan B. I still wanted to have a role in the music industry and I was going to find a plan that would make it work. I renewed my determination to focus on my efforts locally. I began by building a following among a demographic that I could identify with: housewives. My fan base grew from a few moms at my daughters' school to a legion of supporters that I affectionately dub my "minivan mafia", and there's nothing I can't do without their support. Now I sing in and around town fronting a three-piece band known as The Hall Monitors. That's only half the story. In 2008, Waffle House agreed to put my music on their jukeboxes. I secured a distribution and live performance agreement with Walmart.

"In September of 2008 Locals Only debuted on Majic 94.1 out of Lexington, NC. After spending three years pounding the pavement and knocking on doors, I wanted to help other musicians. I approached a local radio station about doing an hour-long show that featured local artists. I've started writing and every summer I teach a songwriting camp for school age kids. Finally, in partnership with the Children's Home Society of North Carolina (www.chsnc.org), I developed a five-month music series that features a different local band each month. We created awareness of both CHS and the local music scene and we raised some money for the Children's Home Society of North Carolina.

"I have a wonderful supportive family. My kids are both school age so I'm able to do a lot of my business during the school day so that the evenings are spent with my family. I've enjoyed the ride, but I've finally found a path that I'm comfortable with, one that lets me be a part-time performer, part-time promoter, and full-time mother."

Would you agree that Lisa Dames is developing her potential and is striving to balance a healthy ego and humility? What an example she is for her growing girls. She deserves a round of applause!

Self-Image

Keep your ego healthy. Your ego is actually your self-image. Your self-image can be an advantage or a disadvantage depending on whether it is positive or negative. That's why it is important to examine your self-image, your ego, to see how it developed, how it is developing, and how you want to see it develop in the future. You think and perform exactly like the type of person you visualize yourself to be. If you are not happy or comfortable with your ego, it is up to you to make the choices that will allow positive changes to happen.

Now for some fun ~

Have you noticed that sometimes you're very logical, sometimes you're thoughtful, and still other times you tend to be emotional? Different people or situations *seem* to turn you into a different person. Enter...Eric Berne, Canadian-born psychologist, who shared with us his *Theory on Transactional Analysis.* Through his intimate research in this area of psychology, Berne was able to discover and explain to us that we are composites of several different "selfs" which emerge according to the time of day, the situation, and the people with whom you are involved. So...we have not just one, not just two, but **three** different selfs that affect our behavior! The more we are aware of the affects of these three different selfs, the better able we will be to effect the changes we want in our lives. Each of these selfs has its own function and projects itself like a voice from within. Although we may not always hear the words, the message will affect our behavior. All three selfs need expression at one time or another, and all play a valuable role in our development as a total person. However, our selfs may sometimes disagree with each other. On the one hand we may "want" to do one thing, while at the same time feeling we "should" do another. This can result in a feeling of internal conflict if we do not understand the interaction between our selfs. Aha! So there *is* an explanation to some of our confusing behaviors! OK! Hold on to your hats…it sounds crazy but we're going "psycho" in this part…

Eric Berne introduced these ego states, these selfs, and their roles in our total being. Allow me to paraphrase his thoughts on these ego states.

The 3 Selfs

One self is **The Parent** and includes all the rules and values you were taught during your early years. This self can be critical, like a father who's disciplining a child, or helpful, like a mother who's helping a young child figure out a puzzle; it is often opinionated and judgmental. Its vocabulary includes restrictive words such as *never, don't,* or *mustn't,* or nurturing words such as *I'll protect you.* This self is your *taught* concept of life. It tells you how you should behave in school, at home, and in society. It also reminds you of what is expected of you. It corresponds with what we were taught to be social norms, and keeps us inside the realm of socially-acceptable behavior. It is often from your Parent ego that you train or discipline children or employees. The Parent self helps you to obey rules, to do what you know is right, and to please others. Listening to this self will often make your journey through life more enjoyable. It is our *taught* concept of life. However, it may embody restrictions that may no longer be appropriate to your current age and conditions, and it could hamper your creativity, imagination, and development.

Here are some indicators of The Parent ego state:

Body language	Expressions	Vocal Tones
Looking down over rim of glasses	"You should... You ought... You must..."	Harsh
Pointing an accusing finger	"Why don't you ever..."	Judgmental
Hands on hips	"Don't tell me..."	Indignant
Head leaning or straining forward	"You disappoint me." "You always..."	Commanding
Patting on back	"Poor thing." "It'll be okay." "Cute, marvelous, awful, childish"	Soothing, Comforting

The Child self is composed of your feelings and emotions. This self includes very natural feelings of joy, sadness, love, and anger. It also includes feelings that you have "learned" as a result of your experiences. Some of these feelings might include feeling inadequate or inferior, or even superior, conforming or withdrawal. When this Child self is in control, your feelings control your behavior. Its vocabulary contains the *I wants, Why nots* and *What the hecks. It's not my fault* and *Did I do OK?* also reflect this self. It tends to be childlike in style. When situations arise where this self can emerge in actual behavior, you can be selfish, demanding, angry, or mean. Or, you can have fun, laugh, cry, love, and generally enjoy yourself. It is your *felt* concept of life.

Here are some indicators of the Child ego state:

Body language	Expressions	Vocal Tones
Forlorn appearance	"I want, I wish..." "Did I do okay?"	Appealing Sullen Worrying

Drooping shoulders	"It's not fair..."	Complaining Indignant
Withdrawal	"It's not my fault..."	Protesting Mumbling
Pursed lips, scowling	"One of these days..."	Grumbling
Skipping, hugging	"Wow! What fun!"	Glee
Cheering, laughing, clapping	"Hurray! Go Team!" "Good for you!"	Happiness

The Adult self is rational and objective, dealing with facts and decisions. It enhances our ability to ask questions, to reason, and to make decisions. Who, what, when, where, and why are words that are included in its vocabulary. This self logically calculates information and makes decisions accordingly. Its tone is conversational and non-threatening. It is your *thought* concept of life.

Here are some indicators of the Adult ego state:

Body language	Expressions	Vocal Tones
A straight relaxed stance	The offer of alternatives and options	Relaxed
Slightly tilted head	The use of the 5 "Ws" in questioning	Assertive
Appearance of active listening	"Aha, I see your point."	Somewhat deliberate
Regular eye contact	"How do you feel about..."	Self-assertive
Confident appearance	"Suitable, recognizable, practical, correct."	Self-confident

One of the keys to success lies in developing an understanding of all three selves. Each of your selves should be in relationship to the total person you want to become. This should play an important role in your personality and success. The role of the logical self is to evaluate the messages from your critical self, together with the feelings from your emotional self, and establish goals and plans which will satisfy all three. It's important that the emotional self want the rewards which the logical self has planned. It's possible the judgmental self will be critical of these plans; be careful to hook the nurturing side of that self. I hope you're not too confused!

In other words, if your critical self is too quick to criticize and too slow to praise, people may not feel free to be open and share things with you. If you are only focused on having fun and not concerned with getting good grades or doing a good job at work, learning, and achieving your goals, you may have a difficult time succeeding. If you are totally logical and unemotional, you will not have the empathy and feeling required to be effective.

While you cannot change some of the circumstances of your development, you can evaluate them, understand them, and overcome any negative influences by learning how to develop thought and behavior processes that are conducive to success.

We come to realize that when we look at the positive sides of the ego states, all have a positive function in our lives. In the Parent ego state resides our values, morals, and realistic limitations which we place on the wants of our Child. The Parent keeps people from going to jail, driving without a license, selling drugs to children, or flunking out of school. The Child is our emotions...our love, laughter, and enjoyment. The Child allows you to laugh, cry, get excited, get angry, and enjoy life. Our Adult is our logic, our thinking, our updating of old tapes. Our Adult helps us to help other people solve their problems, to communicate more effectively, and to become more effective at their jobs. Try not to allow one of your three ego states to stay in control too much. Learn how to focus on the positive aspects of each self.

My study of these ego states as part of the leadership development with Resource Associates Corporation was beneficial in my work helping my clients understand and deal with some of the challenges they faced as they transitioned to college, to internships or to a professional career.

An unknown author shares this version of The Serenity Prayer:

"God grant me the serenity to accept the people I cannot change, the courage to change the one I can, and the wisdom to know it's me!"

Perhaps some of the suggestions in this book will help inspire you to make the choices that are best for you. I challenge you to be bold in your visualizations. Keep in mind that a successful life doesn't just happen. It happens because you plan, set goals and make it happen! You want to hear applause!

What does a successful person look like to you? What are the qualities you perceive a successful person to have developed?

_____

_____

_____

Who do you view as a successful person or as successful people and…why?

_____

_____

Let's look at some past accomplishments or achievements you have reached in your life as you were developing your potential, your ego, your 'self'. List some of your talents and abilities in different areas of your life such as in your social development, your physical development, your mental development, your career and financial development, your home and family life development, and/or your ethics and beliefs development.

Social Development:

_____

_____

Physical Development:

_____

_____

Mental Development:

_____

_____

Career and Financial Development:

_____

_____

Home and Family Life Development:

_____

_____

Ethics and Beliefs Development:

_____

_____

Where are you now with any of them?

_____

_____

_____

Are there any talents and abilities that you would like to develop any further?

_____

_____

_____

Please share with me the areas where you chose to make some improvements. How did this affect you in your personal as well as in your business life?

_____

_____

_____

Please share how others may benefit from this exercise and hear applause?

_____

_____

_____

Have you noticed that healthy doses of self-confidence, self-motivation, self-image, self-love and self-leadership could be wonderful by-products when developing your potential and your ego? This brings us back to the beginning of this chapter when it was mentioned that the original definition of *ego* was "I myself." Ego can certainly be translated as being a positive characteristic of success. Give yourself a round of applause as you boldly and purposefully go about developing a healthy ego.

"Smile" by Charlie Chaplin

Submitted by: Doug Brown, Cranford, New Jersey

"It is an incredibly powerful message that says we can choose how we are going to respond when life throws a disappointment our way. The singer is telling the listener to cheer up and that there is always a brighter tomorrow, especially if we make positive choices and add value to people's lives."

Doug is a process facilitator, consultant, and coach. He provides insight, foresight, and proven processes to professionals in the middle market. He helps develop and align strategy, people, and processes to achieve breakthrough thinking for their real word.

Doug is the chairman/CEO of Paradigm Associates, LLC.

Learn more at: www.ParadigmAssociates.us and/or dbrown@paradigmassociates.us

"Beautiful" by Carole King

Submitted by Michelle Mahalin, Jersey City, NJ

"I can still hear my mom singing this song when I was little. It would make both of us laugh and feel good. Starting my day out with a positive attitude puts me in right frame of mind to deal with whatever challenges I might encounter in my day. Besides, this song just makes me feel empowered and happy. This is how I want my baby to see me – happy, empowered, and helping others feel this way, too."

Michelle is a nurse working for a pharmaceutical company.

Attitude Makes a World of Difference

"I love his positive, can-do attitude!"

"Girl, you have A-T-T-I-T-U-D-E!"

"An attitude like that will get you nowhere fast!"

"He developed such a bad attitude after…"

"Her attitude makes everyone feel like they can succeed."

"Your attitude sucks!"

"Her bossy attitude is such a turnoff."

Attitude is one of those words that have a life of their own. It has presence. It has boldness. It demands responses and reactions, whether positive or negative.

Attitude is crucial to success, and I believe that if you bought this book, you are all…about…success. You probably have ATTITUDE, too! As you can see and hear from the statements at the opening of this chapter, the word *attitude* can take on different meanings depending on the tone of voice, body language, situations, and environments. Some attitudes are assets, and some attitudes are liabilities. Everyone has a little bit of both. An attitude is a tendency to react to people, situations or things in a characteristic way. An attitude is also the way you think and see yourself and the world around you. The experiences in your past and present, and how you view your future life, influence your attitudes. They also influence how you think things should be, how you think people should act, and how you think situations should be handled. Attitude can be quite complicated, as it is tied to experiences and emotions.

Add the fact that your attitude determines the results you get—well, this word and all its trappings can have a real impact on your life. The key to building success attitudes and success habits is in understanding and evaluating what your attitudes are. This will be useful in terms of **your** changing or developing as **you** plan and achieve **your** goals. The good news is that you *do* have a say in developing your attitude and you definitely have the power to use your attitude to your advantage.

Focusing on looking at an attitude change is important. There is a link between attitudes, behavior, and results. It works like this: your attitude about a situation will prompt you to behave or act in a certain way; how you behave will then determine what kind of results you get. My mother used to love saying that a positive attitude may not solve all of your problems, but it will annoy enough people to make it worth the effort!

It's that simple...or not!

Self-Image

As you consciously focus on your positive qualities, you will begin to develop a higher self-image. As your higher self-image grows, so will your ability to achieve your goals and dreams. To a great extent, success is a state of mind.

If your attitude is positive, chances are that you associate with successful, like-minded people—people who are happy, focused, motivated, and who enjoy the fruits of their labor. The fact that they *want* to and actually *do* things to perpetuate success gives them a huge advantage in the game of life. A true positive person doesn't refuse to recognize the negative. He just does not dwell on it.

If your attitude is negative, your behavior will reflect that type of attitude. Giving up, not even trying, being defensive, or avoiding new situations and opportunities, are examples of how *can't* or *won't* ultimately leads to *don't* and therefore missing out on so many opportunities.

Now, a little life lesson on self-image and attitude…

I taught middle school for a number of years, language arts and social studies and also lower level math for "slower" students. To say that the self-image of these particular math students needed some boosting didn't even come close to how they felt about themselves. They considered themselves stupid and losers and failures in the math area. Something just had to be done about that! So I asked questions: "What makes you think you can't do sixth or seventh grade math? How does that make you feel?" Some of the answers I got were something like these: Too many numbers. Just too hard. Not good in math. Problems too hard to understand…

Then I asked them about when in their life they started feeling they could not be successful in math. Most mentioned that it was after the third grade. Interesting, I thought. This bit of information caused me to rethink my approach to teaching math concepts to my students. Before each new unit or chapter for my math lessons, without them knowing it, I would start out by using the work from a third-grade math book and proceeded to put the work on the board and asked them to solve it. They could do this! If they couldn't, it was far easier to teach them at a basic level than to teach them at grade level. Then I would go to a fourth-grade math book and do the same. They could do this! I would then take a fifth- grade math book and do the same. They could do it! Then I would go into the sixth- or seventh-grade lesson. Now that my students' perception of themselves was so much more positive, they would be able to work the activities in the math book at the appropriate grade level. Wow! When my students realized that pretty much most of the time, moving to a higher level in math was just adding more numbers to the knowledge that they already had learned in a lower grade, they were much more willing and able to do the work. If it was an altogether new math concept, the students now tackled the challenge with a more positive attitude. Grades went from Fs and Ds and Cs to Bs and even As! They also enjoyed becoming tutors for third-graders once a week after school. They never thought that *they* could be tutors…after all, you had to be smart to be a tutor! And to add icing to the cake, my students even passed the End of Year Math tests at or above grade level! This was a first for these students. Did they hear applause? You can be sure they did.

This is a method that can be used by parents when working through challenging math problems and activities with their children. As a matter of fact, it can successfully be implemented in just about any case, whether it is at school, in sports, at home, or at work. Don't be afraid to break it down to the basics, and then when the basics are mastered and the self-esteem and positive attitude are in place, gradually increase the level of difficulty until they get to the level that needs to be attained. No sense rushing it. Take it one step at a time. Everyone will reap the rewards of positive self-esteem and mastery of a challenging task.

Now on a business level…

A few years ago, my friend Linda Blumenfeld never had thought she'd be saying, "I'm fabulous at fifty!" Here she is to share her change of attitude:

Linda Blumenfeld

"I'm excited about the future. I'm not afraid to take chances with other people that I trust and have close personal and or professional bonds with. They are helping me learn who I am at fifty and encouraging me to be 'fabulous at fifty!'

"Let's go back a "few" years, when I was a young twenty-something in Fort Lauderdale, Florida. I love people and fashion, and marketing has always been one of my passions. A friend of mine was an artist who designed and hand painted clothing. She asked me to market her fashions. I was in college and needed money and a job, and this was certainly a unique product to market. I accepted the challenge. I found I had a talent for this and quickly built up eighty accounts in the Southeast area of the United States, some in very prestigious stores. It took me to several states. We were quite a successful team. It was pretty exciting!

"Then I met this guy, Larry Blumenfeld, and he swept me off my feet. Before we knew it, we were married and started our wonderful family. My career in marketing, as well as my college career, was put on hold while this phase of my life took front and center stage; however, it was always in the back of my mind. It was my choice to be a stay-at-home mom, and I loved it. Yet as the children grew up and the budget needed a little boost, I found an outlet for my creativity and marketing and started Parties by Linda. For several years one could find me at children's parties on weekends, where I designed a theme party for an event. That was fun!

"The children were now really growing up, high school and college, and now I found that I had the freedom to pursue my passion! But doubts did start to nag at me; after all, I did not have a college degree. Who would hire me for real? My strengths of creativity, confidence, enthusiasm, daring, high energy, unselfishness, and organization, as well as the ability to form strong relationships with business associates, friends, and family saved the day. I am a *can-do* woman with a very positive attitude. I reflected back on how I made my creativity and my marketing talents work for me in the past. I worked with a coach to list all the positives that I could bring to a company, even if I didn't have that college degree. I listed the results of my efforts. Aha! A ***paradigm shift!*** People pay for ***results***...not necessarily all the degrees and letters that come after your name! It doesn't matter how many degrees or certifications you have: if you can't produce the results your client is looking for, you will soon find yourself without work. Well...I was proud to see that my past customers were quite happy with the results they got by hiring me to do their events. Plus, the fact that they referred my services to others spoke volumes of the quality of the work I did. With this information, my self-confidence improved and I did start applying for marketing jobs. For the past three years I have been very successful at marketing for a regional women's magazine. I have found that my marketing talents and skills have helped my friends and clients succeed in their businesses. They were getting results by having me help with their marketing. You see, I truly believe that it's really not just about me—it really is about *them* and *their* business. I have renewing clients/customers and a steady paycheck, one I can be proud of, even though this is payment on commission.

"My husband of 25 years, yes, my sweetheart, Larry, is now encouraging me go out on my own. Wow! He believes that there is no reason why I can't have my own company and market the way I would love to do. And...I finally agree with him! It is now time to do marketing for myself! I am not going back; I'm going forward in a positive direction for me and for others in the community. This quote inspires me: 'What would you attempt to do if you knew you could not fail.' (Unknown) I have the confidence and the ability to succeed in my business. What a feeling!"

Congratulations to Linda! It'll be quite something to watch this whirlwind take the marketing business by storm. Let's give her a round of applause!

Choose to discover what's inside you and what motivates you. Find your purpose and intention and that will act as a compass as you rise up to your dreams. Know why you want certain things, how you can get them, when you can get them, and the results of all when it happens because of your choices. Stop making excuses. Make decisions based on **your** talents, **your** strengths, **your** life, **your** job, **your** passions, **your** priorities, and how this contributes to **your** goals. As you work on your strengths, this will help you know what motivates you. The more motivated **you** are, the better chances you have on staying focused and on track. Chances are you will be more energized and get things done in a more positive manner. Smiling even. Who wouldda thought? Purpose, intention, and motivation help you feel more in control of yourself. They allow you be more deliberate in your decisions. How can you not help but be successful and hear that applause?

What should you allow in your life? How can it make your life different and better? Can it add value to your life? And this goes without saying that this will have a ripple effect on others around you.

Remember, also, the value of **quality**. Do not settle for anything but your best, nothing less. Aim at excelling in what you choose to do. In all activities, especially those related to your visions and dreams, put your best foot forward. Excellence opens the door to even more possibilities. As you strive to do your best at honing your skills and mastering new skills, you will find that it is much easier to reach your goals because you have created an expectation of achievement. Keep in mind that **you are no ordinary person: you are extraordinary** and well on your way to success. Only the best for you!

Developing a positive, winning attitude requires daily effort. It requires that every day you choose to take the responsibility to put positive input into your mind. Negatives attract failure. Positives attract success. You choose to learn and find ways and opportunities that will allow you to strengthen the attitudes that will lead you to success. You do not want to be a victim. You want to choose to be to be a change agent, a doer, a hero for yourself and others.

Remember how I said at the beginning of the book that even *I* have to work at being positive and thinking with a solution in mind? Let me share something that happened to me recently at a conference I was attending. This conference of about three thousand ladies was held at a BIG hotel and conference center.

This was in Texas and everything is BIG in Texas! The room where the meals and snacks were served was a good distance from the rooms where the workshops and presentations were being made. I felt like I was walking-running in a marathon just to get some food and hightail it back to the conference area to keep on the schedule the organizers had set up for us. I was tired, hot, and getting kind of cranky. Yes, I was thinking negative thoughts: Why did they put the food sooooo far away from everything? We have to rush so much. We will have a hard time getting our food and then getting a seat. And we have to carry all our stuff back and forth. Yes...I WAS getting cranky. But then I thought: "OK, Leona, get over it, already! How can I make this work?" I starting to thank the conference organizers (in my mind) for being so thoughtful and for the opportunity to power walk and get some exercise after sitting for such long sessions. Then I decided to put all my materials down on a chair at the end of a row of seats—or at least on a seat in the back of the next room that I would be sitting in—before I went to get my lunch or a snack. Now my hands were free to get my lunch or my snack, and I could inconspicuously slip into the workshop with my food and enjoy the presentation. Power walking had me walking taller, faster, and smiling more at myself for being proactive. This positive thinking worked quite well for me from then on and I certainly did have fun sharing this solution with many ladies. It made a lot of people laugh and start to think of ways that we can make things works in our favor. I chose to take positive action. I chose to make positive actions, thoughts, and words part of my success process.

Surround yourself with positive things as much as you can, all the time, if possible. Be conscious of the choices you make. Keep in mind that your attitude not only affects you, but affects others around you. Developing winning attitudes requires daily effort. It requires that each day you put some positive input in your mind. Through a regular reading program, (which includes positive, growth-oriented, self-improvement books and articles), daily listening to self-improvement tapes or CDs, and a daily focus on goals, you will nourish positive attitudes. Even bedtime reading should be positive, because research has shown that even what you read before bed or going to sleep is reinforced and kept in your mind.

Take time to do things as a family or work unit. Have weekly, informal meetings, where everyone shares the positives and negatives of their week; they can have input on family or work matters and feel safe to ask for advice and solutions to challenges they face. Everyone is worth this effort. A strong sense of caring and love and security is formed and can be a catalyst for members to make positive decisions. If a mistake is made, the members can feel the support necessary to right that mistake and not feel that they lose face. Valuable skills like communication and critical thinking and active listening can be developed that will impact many other areas of their lives. In our family, Monday night was our family night. Monday seemed to be the night when there were no sports or music lessons, and Dad was pretty much in town and not away on business. We valued that night. We would have our family discussions, catch up on what each of us was doing, and then play games or watch a movie together. Our kids are grown now and they still talk about Monday Family Nights.

If you are choosing to improve your life by improving your attitude, you are probably aware that all new experiences and changes come with some degree of anxiety, doubt, or fear. That's a normal reaction and could make you a bit resistant to change. Awareness of some obstacles that could be overcome will set you up for success.

F.E.A.R

Many people allow **fear** to be the determining factor when trying new things. Fear is not a four letter word. Fear can bog you down and prevent you from accomplishing anything, or fear can be the catalyst to challenging yourself to attempt something new. You've probably heard or read that **fear** is simply: **F**alse **E**xpectations **A**ppearing **R**eal. Notice the two words *false* and *appearing.* Would you agree that these two words take some of the wind out of one's sails when it comes to dealing with fear? I am not discounting that fear of the unknown can be a powerful negative force. After all, if we choose to change, we may not be certain of the results we will get.

Let's think of the benefits of fear. I know: fear and benefits in the same sentence…Yeah! Right!

Sure! Think about it for a moment. Fear offers you choices, challenges you, cultivates your faith in yourself and others, and helps you grow. What if we re-educate our subconscious and shift our feeling of fear to one of challenge or excitement? What if we use fear as a green light to…GO—to try, to consider, like: "I'm onto something big, here!" You can build the momentum by putting positive actions into place and then…GO for it.

Jacqueline Wales, author of *The Fearless Factor*, will help put this in perspective: "Being fearless is not the absence of fear but the choices and decisions we make when fear shows up in our lives."

My amazing friend Susan Midgett certainly had her set of fears to deal with after she made a life-changing decision…a life-changing decision that would affect not only her and her family, but would affect hundreds of children in Haiti. Here's Susan to share her adventure with you:

Susan Midgett

"In August 2009, I swallowed my fear and jumped into the San Francisco Bay along with approximately seven hundred other swimmers, none of which I personally knew. My initial purpose was to complete the *17th Annual Escape from Alcatraz Sharkfest Swim*, and my first open-water swim in the ocean. *Sharkfest* is roughly a mile-and-a half swim—more like two miles when it's all said and done—that begins with a leap from a ferry just off the shores of Alcatraz Island, and terminates on the shores of San Francisco,

California. The 58-degree water was a surprising shock to the body that added anxiety even with the prior knowledge it was going to be extremely cold. The currents and ebb tide were definitely in play, as I had to swim in a direction almost opposite where I wanted to finish. And then there was the issue of unknown sea creatures lurking beneath! Did I have some fear? Sure. But, I carried with me the support and blessings of family and friends, faith that God was watching over me, and most importantly, the *purpose* of my swim. I wasn't just swimming for the satisfaction of personal accomplishment—there was a greater reason—and that's where the real scary part comes in.

"Some months prior, I had an inspired idea to merge my desire to complete the Alcatraz swim as a physical challenge with my passion for raising awareness and helping the people, especially the children, in the tiny country of Haiti. This was well before the 2010 earthquake, and the situation in Haiti seemed quite overlooked to me. So, I decided to create a fundraiser, that I dubbed *S.O.S. for Haiti*, and use the swim to attempt to raise $100,000—during the worst economy in decades, as it turned out—for a medical/dental clinic at *Pwoje Espwa* (Project Hope), in Les Cayes, Haiti. But, just like the Alcatraz Swim, I had no prior experience at raising such a large sum of money, so this was a huge part of the whole endeavor that greatly added to my fear. Could I really accomplish what I telling people I was going to do? It was most important to me that I could, and the question often kept me awake at night.

"In March 2009, I traveled to Haiti and I was even more inspired by the needs I witnessed first-hand, as well as the difference Father Marc Boisvert, the founder of *Pwoje Espwa Sud*, and the many wonderful volunteers of the supporting non-profit organization, Theo's Work, Inc. (www.freethekids.org), had made in the lives of thousands. In Haiti, poverty takes on a whole new meaning. Starvation is so common that many parents choose to abandon their children, or they are duped into giving them away in hopes they will have a better life, but it's often child-slavery in disguise. *Pwoje Espwa* provides housing, food, education and basic medical care for more than eight hundred of these orphaned or abandoned children which transforms, and in many cases literally saves, their lives.

"The conditions in Haiti were difficult, and experiencing it first hand was life-changing. Being able to see in person the faces of the children, and receive their unconditional hugs, sealed my resolve to help them. They were beautiful children who happened to be born in a country with wretched conditions. Despite my fears, it was my hope that through my Alcatraz swim, I could make a difference by raising the huge sum necessary for a new medical clinic desperately needed at the orphanage. The current clinic is small and inadequate which only allows for rudimentary care to be given. With an expanded facility, more needless suffering in Haiti will be eliminated. There will be space for an overnight infirmary for sick children, an X-ray room, a treatment area for minor surgery, an adequate lab, and for the first time ever in the vicinity — a dental clinic and an area for public health education. But most importantly, the new clinic will allow for the comprehensive care that ultimately will make it possible for more children to reside at *Pwoje Espwa*, rescuing them from their desperate living conditions.

"So, was I afraid, worried about failure, and thinking twice about what I was committing to do? Absolutely. I knew this endeavor would cause me to go WAY out of my comfort zone and require me to 'put myself out there' and do things I previously avoided whenever I could, like public speaking, asking people to donate money, traveling to unstable parts of the world, and even swimming in really cold water with the possibility of sharks. But, I had faith in God that somehow it would all work out. I just tried to focus on what life is like for so many of the children in Haiti, and the grim outlook especially for the ones trapped in a life of slavery. Eventually, my anxieties and second thoughts would fade. There is no comparing my fears to what the children in Haiti endure every day."

Fear…absolutely. Positive attitude and faith…yes. Putting a plan into action…a necessity. Family and community support… with pride. Success…absolutely!

Susan's goal when she began her quest was to raise $100,000, and by the time she was in the bay swimming five months later —yes, that's right—*only five months later*, in August 2009—she had already raised over $82,000! And…believe it or not…she actually reached her goal in just nine months—total! Amazing! Yet, her challenge has only just begun. The recent earthquake has made the needs in Haiti and at *Pwoje Espwa* even greater. She plans to continue her work to help. Wow! Susan is one of my "sheroes."

Wouldn't you agree that she definitely deserves a round of applause…probably even a standing ovation?!

If you are interested in learning more about *Pwoje Espwa* or *S.O.S. for Haiti*, please visit: www.freethekids.org and/or www.sosforhaiti.blogspot.com.

If you still experience fear of the unknown, try writing down all possible outcomes, listing both negative and positive ones. Look at the list carefully. Are the negative outcomes you fear really that horrible? Are the positive outcomes exciting enough to motivate you to change? If they are, highlight them, set them as goals. Put them in a prominent place, on the refrigerator, on your dresser, in your locker, on your car visor… and **just do it!**

Change reflects growth, and growth can bring about conflicting emotions about things you were comfortable with in the past. However, you now see that changes *must* be made if you want to reach the levels of success and personal power you desire. You may experience *conflict* with people in your lives, or conflict with thoughts that have been a part of your daily regimen, or conflict with your new emotions and aspirations. People might question you and make you second guess yourself. Maybe others are a little envious of your new self-development. These are new experiences, and you need to build your comfort level as you choose ways to be more successful.

Most people don't enjoy confrontational situations. "Help me understand…" is the best opening phrase I know of to use or say when you disagree with someone's perspective or are in judgment, and vice versa. It comes across as conversational and non-threatening. It opens the door for more positive communication.

If conflict is an obstacle you might be facing, become comfortable with words or phrases you will need to use by practicing them over and over until you can comfortably say them. This helps you over this hurdle.

People who have no goals or direction can develop a *laissez-faire* kind of attitude. They may be constantly busy, always moving, but going around in circles, never arriving, never achieving. It is *busy-ness* vs. *business*, whether the business is a career, job, activity or school. How frustrating this must be! To deflect this **lack of purpose**, one needs to have focus and a game plan. This is where goal planning and successful execution of those plans come into play. A step-by-step plan can be the tool you need as you attempt your new change of attitude.

YOU are your attitude and your attitude precedes you in your world. It is your calling card to success and opening doors of opportunity.

Changing your attitude also requires you to take an "inside-out" look at yourself.

I asked my daughter-in-law, Kate, to share an excerpt from the journal she kept while in Ethiopia. She and my son Dan were volunteering for a year serving as a medical and social working team for the independent organization Lalmda (my son is doctor and Kate has a master's degree in social work). This was towards the end of their year there. They had experienced an incredible amount of happiness as well as stress in their daily dealings with the challenges of this third-world country.

"Six weeks to go, in Ethiopia, and I should be *left*...reflecting on my experience here (what I have learned and how I have grown) but instead I find myself *left* with lots of work.

"Dan and Carrole (our new Project Director) have gone to Jimma to get meds, petroleum and other stuff. I am 'holding down the fort' for a few days. This means I am operating as the Medical Director, Project Director, Children's Home and Outreach Coordinator and ambulance driver.

"Yesterday I had a horrible headache and amoeba again (an amoeba is a kind of parasitic infection resembling acute flu-like symptoms)...I struggled through the tasks, of all these positions, until I retired to bed around 8:00. I was beat, to say the least.

"This morning I woke up...not ready for the day ahead. I stumbled over to our common house to make myself a pot of coffee (usually this is a part of Dan's morning ritual). It was very quiet, very serene and as my senses came alive, I realized that I needed to enjoy this morning of solitude (before the staff arrived and the clinic opened).

"I sat on our back porch (in my pjs) with a boiling pot of water, my coffee cup, and the filter system we used to make the coffee. I listened to the noises of the morning (a rooster, a monkey, birds, and the grinding mill)...and poured hot water continually through the coffee system.

"I decided that I wouldn't let the day overwhelm me. I would take the time to sit and enjoy my cup of warm coffee and absorb the beauty of the morning.

"Actually, I was absorbed in the coffee making...still listening to the sounds, but not 'opening' my eyes.

"As I poured my cup of coffee and lifted my head to 'see' the beauty of the day, a beautiful, full-spectrum rainbow emerged right in front of my eyes. It was magnificent! I could not have created a more perfect place to 'take in' the morning.

"It was as if God said to me, 'Kate, take the time to appreciate my beauty and I will reveal amazing things.'

"I guess I just wanted to share this little story because I believe that tiny miracles happen around us every day and we just don't take the time to notice them. Today, stop for a moment and let the universe reveal itself to you...

Peace, Kate"

Wow! Taking the time for an "attitude adjustment" before another challenging day helped Kate become calmer and now she was better prepared to deal with her responsibilities. She deserves a round of applause for sharing this experience with us. Thanks, Kate!

If you are interested in learning more about Lalmba, the "World's Smallest Relief Agency," a "place of hope," please visit: www.lalmba.org

It is a lot easier to change yourself than to change others. Ideally, people will notice your positive changes and your positive attitude and will be inspired to follow your example.

Mahatma Gandhi said, "You must be the change you want to see in the world."

Are you up to the challenge? Do you believe that you are worth it? I think I Hear Applause!

List seven things that you enjoy doing. What is your attitude as you are doing them? Is it positive? Does it make you happy? Do you procrastinate when it is time to do these activities?

_____

_____

_____

List seven things that you do not enjoy doing.

_____

_____

_____

What is your attitude as you are doing these? Is it positive? Does it make you happy? Do you procrastinate when it is time to do them?

_____

_____

Are you ready for an *attitude adjustment*? Is there a particular attitude that needs some work? What will you do about it?

_____

_____

Please share with me a time when you treated yourself to an "attitude adjustment. What difference did it make to your day? Did it make a difference in someone else's day? Did you hear applause?

_____

_____

_____

"What About Everything?" by Carbon Leaf

Submitted by Nicole Leger, Dorchester, Massachusetts

"In our modern, fast-paced world there are a lot of little things in life that may aggravate us and maybe even make us stumble down the path of life. This song helps to reevaluate your situation and makes you remember to take a moment to look at the big picture. Don't sweat the small stuff!"

Nicole is a paralegal.

"Allahalek Ya Sidi" from the album Truly by Ishtar

Submitted by Sharon Eden, London, England

"I don't understand a word of this song from Ishtar, a Middle Eastern singing star, but the beat, energy, and sounds get my hips wiggling…and before long, my funk is yesterday's news!"

Sharon is an Inner Leadership Coach who helps leaders with dispirited executives find their purpose, passion, and power at work - right now.

Learn more at: www.sharoneden.biz and/or
sharon.eden@womenofcourage.co.uk

Reframe, Redo, Recover

No! This chapter is *not* about decorating! It's about changing old ways of thinking about things. You will be challenged to substitute empowering thoughts or words in place of disempowering ones. We will be doing some **paradigm shifting.** Reframing, redoing, and recovering means using innovative thinking, creative thinking, and possibly some good old-fashioned psychological thinking that will encourage you to express yourself in ways that will give you more ROI—Return On Investment—on your emotional deposits. When we deposit money in the bank or in any money-raising account, we expect it to grow and flourish. It is the same with people. If we deposit good, empowering words, phrases, or suggestions with them, they will also grow and flourish and increase in value.

Reframing

In their book, ***100 Ways to Build Self-Esteem***, Diane Loomans and Julia Loomans share with us that reframing, redoing or recovering is based on using positive words and phrases to get a desired effect. Yes, there are more optimistic ways of dealing with life's little hiccups: disgruntled teens, unruly children, unappreciative friends, stubborn employees...you know some of the people I'm alluding to. Also, Susan Wilson Solovic adds her suggestions for some positive, impactful changes in her book: ***The Girls' Guide to Power & Success***. Use these success skills as templates to evoke positive responses, reactions, and participation. I don't pretend that using these techniques will be like waving a magic wand and everything will be just wonderful; after all we are dealing with real life, with real people. However, the techniques can certainly make life easier for all involved. They are not intended to deny negative actions and emotions that might require understanding and empathy. But they will give us a chance to deal with situations in a more pleasant manner. You will see that it is worth the effort. I will add some of their suggestions to mine, as I paraphrase some of the suggestions in their books.

It will take practice. You will need to get used to new ways of approaching this train of thought. It will take practice because people might just think you've gone a little loony on them because you are choosing to use more unorthodox approaches.

You should start feeling a certain sense of control over situations, getting the results you are striving for and expecting. You might also start noticing certain feelings of renewed respect and calm as you all are responding differently to this method of communication.

When these success strategies are done right, your tone of voice should be conversational, non-threatening, yet directed. And...by the way...a smile really helps!

I know—Enough explanation! Let's get to it!

Let's start with some typical sayings and some **possible reframing examples**; who knows—there could also be some invisible goals.

* RF = Reframing

* IG = Invisible goal

* **"Look at the time! Hurry up or we'll be late!"**
 RF: "What can we do so that we will be on time?"
 (To get things rolling, someone might have to start on the thought process...Tim...Mike...Sue... Or you might need to be a little more

specific, especially at the beginning…Tim, please put the dog in the kennel…Sue, please put your sister's sweater on her…Good job…we're getting closer to being on time!)

IG: *Respect, developing responsibility, cooperation, thinking skills, stating the goal of being on time.*

* "Pets can be so annoying!"

RF: *"As much as we love our pets, sometimes they do seem to have an amazing ability to seek attention and be noticed, don't they? Please give me a moment to see if I can calm Rover down."*

IG: *Acknowledged the person's annoyance, affirmed the importance of pets in our family (especially in front of the children), realizing that it was the situation that needed to be addressed.*

* "Oh man! I have so much work to do"

RF: *"OK…I need to get started. Should I begin with the work I enjoy the most or the work I enjoy the least?"*

IG: *Motivation, prioritization, action.*

Sometimes just having a repertoire of **funny or unusual words or phrases** that can be used is enough to break the negativity… even though you are saying the same thing, but in a more tempered way.

We can take a cue from Dr. Seuss: "I like nonsense. It wakes up the brain cells!"

With that in mind, here are some examples:

* "I'm really tired."
RF: *"Looks like it's time to recharge my batteries."*

* "This place is a mess!"
RF: *"If a burglar came to rob our house right now, he'd leave because it looks like it's been ransacked!"*

* "I'm really angry!"

RF: *"Bet you can see the smoke coming out of my ears!"*

* **"Please do not be so rude."**
RF: *"Why are you being so cheeky and supercilious?"*

Secret Signs/Signals

Have some secret signs/signals or cues that you can use with other people.

If an action or activity needs to be addressed because it is making you uncomfortable or perhaps you feel a need for improvement, devising a secret code or signal to help them is caring and respectful. For instance, my husband was concerned that people might get annoyed with my enthusiasm and my jumping in at any time in a conversation or worse, just taking over the conversation. He mentioned this to me, and although I was embarrassed at first, I realized he was doing this because he cared. We devised a signal of his pulling at his earlobe when I needed to tone it down, or if he was sitting next to me, just a light touch on my leg to make me aware of what I was doing. It was our own signal and I felt respected and loved.

When I was growing up, asking my mother to have a cup of tea with me signaled to her that I needed some alone time with her to talk about something that was important to me. This also gave her time to finish what she was doing and get mentally prepared talk with me. This was quite successful, and I continued that tradition with my own children as they were growing up. Even now my daughters will laugh when we are on the phone and say that it is time for a cup of tea if there's an issue that needs more attention.

When my son was in middle school, he did not appreciate hugs and kisses as I dropped him off at school: understandable. So we used the Hawaiian hello sign as a way of saying, "Goodbye...I love you." and that was acceptable for a middle-school person.

Say What You Want

Learn to say what you want, not what you don't want.

We have been programmed to emphasize what we don't want rather than what we do want, and then we wonder why there is a communication gap. Since people tend to respond to the message they are hearing, the words need to match what you want to happen. The brain visualizes what you say as it acts on the request or statement. For instance, if you tell someone, "Don't slam the door," the door will probably slam shut. The brain heard *slam the door*, registered that message, so the result was slamming the door. The chances for the desired outcome would be more achievable if it was phrased like, "Please close the door gently." or "Please hold onto the door so it closes quietly." The brain hears *close gently, close quietly*, registers that message, and chances are the door will close gently or quietly.

Other examples:

* "Get your feet off the coffee table"
RF: "Please put your feet down on the carpet."

* "Whatever you do, don't come home late after school today."
RF: "I know that I can count on you to be home by 4 today after school."

* "Oh yes…Pick up the cake and ice cream on your way home. Don't forget, now!"
RF: "Remember to get the cake and ice cream on your way home. Thanks!"

On a flight a few weeks ago from New York to Greensboro, there was a young mother with a tot on her lap. The little boy kept kicking the seat in front of him and the mother kept telling him to stop the kicking. He was not stopping and the mother was getting a bit exasperated. I asked permission, then, quietly mentioned to the little boy that when we are on a plane the plane flies better if people keep their feet still. So, he should keep his feet still. Could he keep his feet still for us? He smiled, looked at his feet, and stopped kicking. I thanked him for being such a good boy. His mom was happy and asked how I did that. I mentioned how telling him what she wanted him to do (keep his feet still), perhaps repeating the desired action or response a few times, would usually produce the intended results. A thank you with a smile goes a long way, too.

Offer Focused Feedback

When you offer feedback, focus on the behavior, not on the person. This prevents a sense of entitlement by taking the focus off the person and putting it on the activity or project. Avoid saying something like, "You're such a pro in the customer service department." Instead focus on the activity: "I admire you for keeping calm with that irate customer and not reacting to his anger." This type of feedback will remind the employee how valuable his service is and how he should continue this type of positive action.

"You are such a nice person," could be restated as: "Jake, Mrs. Smith mentioned how thoughtful you were to shovel the snow for her. She really appreciates it."

Say What You Really Mean

Isn't it annoying when you have to second-guess what someone is asking or telling you? How often do you find yourself beating around the bush instead of just saying what you really mean up front? Or maybe it's because you want to be "cute" or evasive? It could be fear or insecurity that causes us to do this. It could be that it might just take more effort than you really want to put into it. But since we are on the path of being more self-confident and more assertive, the area of indirect statements is one that should be addressed. Would you agree with me that someone could become upset, or angry, or confused because you are "afraid" to say whatever you need to say because you don't want to make them angry or upset? Some of the success strategies we are looking at developing are some that encourage thinking skills and communication skills. Practicing what you want to say ahead of time is one of them. Do this whenever possible.

For example:

* Indirect statement: "Wouldn't it be nice if the family room looked neater?"

Desired response: Someone will help you straighten up the family room.

Direct statement: *"Sue, please hang up your coat. Pete, please straighten up your computer games. Johnny, please bring the snacks to the kitchen and put them away."*

* Indirect statement: "It would probably be a good idea to have extra copies of this report."

Desired response: Someone will offer to go make copies.

Direct statement: *"Please make 10 additional copies of this report and bring them to our morning meeting."*

* Indirect statement: "It's hot in here."

Desired response: Someone will offer to open a window or adjust a thermostat.

Direct: *"I'm hot. John, would you please open a window?"*

Keeping feelings and situations in perspective when choosing to be more direct and straightforward in your communication, will command more respect for you and from you. It saves time, money, and feelings. It's more professional.

Imagine what impact this could have with your relationships at work, at school, and with your family? Do you think people would be less misunderstood?

Changing One Word

Just changing one word in a sentence can pack a powerful punch.

* Let's change the word *but* to *and*—or—*but* to *next time.*

"Jim, I like what you did with this proposal, but you could have added more details to make it more convincing."

The *but* negated or erased the compliment and probably had Jim wondering if his supervisor was actually disappointed in his performance. The *but* probably was said without a smile and tended to sound a bit bossy.

* Now let's switch the *but* with *and/ next time.*

"Jim, I like what you did with this proposal; thanks. And next time, adding more details will make it more convincing."

The *and* was much friendlier and softens the criticism. Jim is probably thinking his supervisor appreciated his work and that he has confidence that there will be other proposals he will be expected to work on. This was probably said with a smile. This is also more future-oriented and lets Jim know that he will have other opportunities to improve.

* Let's change *if* to *when.*

"If I get a chance to finish that paper, I will be so relieved."

This is now iffy…it looks like this person might be looking for an excuse. There is probably a lack of commitment to the project.

* Now let's switch the *if* to *when.*

"When I finish that paper, I will be so relieved."

There is a sense of commitment to the project, a belief that it will get done. That person is challenging himself to see it through.

Now let's transform the **What ifs…**into **What can I…**

"What ifs" create negative thinking patterns and uncertainty. They are roadblocks to success. When you start *What-if-ing* yourself or others, just stop and switch back to *"How can I…"*

You will notice your confidence increasing and more goals being met.

For example:

"What if she says no to my asking for a raise?"

Think: How can I position myself to show that I am worthy of that raise? How can I stay calm and positive during our meeting?

With our company, The Lattitude Group, we've chosen to say that we've "opened" business when we get a new contract, rather than say that we've "closed" business. The word "closed" leaves us with the feeling that there is nothing more that has to be done now; we've clinched it and it kind of leaves us with a smug feeling. Our choice to use "open" challenges us to be ready for new opportunities and to help this new client successfully reach his goals. It gives us permission to be as professional and creative as we need to be so our client gets a great ROI.

Are there any other simple word changes that could be made when thinking of reframing for appreciation, motivation, or developing self-esteem?

_____

_____

_____

Here are a couple more examples of how an intentional use of words can make a world of difference in how your message is received and understood:

Mother Theresa was once asked to speak at an anti-war rally and she refused. "If it was a pro-peace rally, I would attend," she explained. "But fighting against a war, or fighting against anything, is just another form of war." She believed in peace.

On a lighter note: "A foolish man tells a woman to stop talking, but a wise man tells a woman that her mouth is extremely beautiful when her lips are closed." This man also believes in peace!

Eliminating Words

Eliminating particular words can send a stronger message.

Using the words *just* and *only* can diminish the professionalism and importance of a message.

* Using *just*:

"Hi Debbie! It's *just* Lee and I would *just* like to talk to you about setting an appointment to talk with me next week about something to do with your college..."

The receiver of this call probably is thinking...Oh great... what is it she wants now and how long is this *really* going to take if I do return her call...

A possible rephrase could be: "Hi Debbie! This is Leona La Perriere with LATTITUDE 4 U. I hope all is well with you. Summer will be over before we know it, and students will be back in school. Debbie, I'm calling to set an appointment to discuss some new ideas that could increase the retention rate at your university. Here are some dates that I have available as of today...."

* Using *only*:

"Hi Sue! It's *only* me, Lee, and I *only* want to tell you about..."

A possible rephrase could be:

"Hi Sue! This is Leona La Perriere with LATTITUDE 4 U. I hope all is well with you. I know how proud you must be with your daughter Jill having graduated from high school last week. Congratulations! Sue, I am excited about our new college success process that can make a difference in how Jill could experience a more positive transition to college this year. Here are some dates that I have available as of today to discuss this new process…"

These examples were short, professional, friendly, and specific.

It takes practice to eliminate the words "just" and "only"; however you will sound much more professional if you can do this.

Adding… "OK?" or "All right?"

When making a statement, especially to a younger person such as a child (actually, even to an adult), adding *OK? or All right?* at the end of the statement diffuses the intent of the statement and can also add confusion to the listener. It's like asking permission or unintentionally giving them doubt to what you are saying. Most of us say this to soften the statement or order, or to make it sound like we want agreement, but it often adds confusion instead. The listener probably thinks that he has a choice to do what was requested or not to do it. For instance:

* "John, please finish your homework so we can go out, OK?"

The speaker has already asked nicely (please) so it would have more impact to simply stop the request at "out."

This is a harder habit to change; however, one will most probably get better results.

Another way to get a desired response when wanting to be sure the message is understood without saying *OK or all right*, could be something like this:

* "I want to make sure that I communicated clearly to you. Would you please tell me what you heard...what you plan to do..."

This is less condescending, more clarifying, and more professional.

Now let's look at the work *try.*

When used in a statement, the work *try* lessens the meaning of the action being attempted. It implies the possibility of failure, of not owning up to something, or of possibly not giving it your best shot. It is regarded as an escape mechanism that one can use as an excuse for not getting it done.

Really now...It's either you do it...or you don't.

* "I'll try to practice my piano lesson." or "I'll try to study hard so that I can pass that test." or "I'll try get to the store before it closes"

It's almost like you're setting yourself up for failure and using **try** as an excuse for not succeeding.

Change the **try** to **will** and see the difference in the results you will get.

* "I will practice my piano lesson today." or "I will study hard so that I can pass that test." or "I will get to the store before it closes."

Now you are setting yourself up for success and your brain will now be able to think about ways to make it happen. You now become pro-active in reaching your goal.

I think you're starting to get the gist of this. Reframing can be used successfully with news headlines, quotations, slogans, and stories, too. You can make a game out of this or have a contest. Yes, it can be used in positive and fun ways. The more positive you think and are about things, the more positive your life becomes.

While we are on the topic…

It is very important to always tell your spouse, your significant other, your kids, your parents, your family members, your friends WHY you love them. Telling them you love them is very important. Reframing this by adding the magic ingredient of the WHY makes it much more special: you've taken the time to really notice, you appreciate them as individuals, and that they are important to you. This can be done by pointing out something specific about them, what they did, or what they took part in. Doing this shows that you are really paying attention. What an incredible compliment that is to anyone! Would you agree that this could lead to positive behavior patterns that will benefit everyone? It **is** really worth the extra effort!

My friend Sue Falcone, known as "Simply Sue, A Speaker Who Writes", realized at a later stage and age, that she could *reframe* her life. Here's her story:

"Simply" Sue

"Born illegitimate, in crisis, and not expected to live, I faced many life challenges beginning from birth. I journeyed through abuse, neglect, divorce, single parenting, and step-parenting. I made bad choices, had many broken relationships, and never seemed to find the joy, peace and contentment that I longed for. I was blessed with a wonderful corporate career with numerous rewards and successes and an awesome family, but the thoughts of not being "good enough" or worthy of value kept me from my dream of being a speaker who writes. Then after hitting rock bottom twelve years ago, heavily overweight, deeply in debt, with no plan or income in sight, I finally had come to the end of myself. I gave in totally to God and with His help He showed me how to *reframe* my life and become the author of

The Lighthouse of Hope—A Day by Day Journey to Fear Free Living. By facing and overcoming my fears I am now an international motivational and inspirational speaker and writer. I am living my dream and helping others see that they can, too"

You should see the applause Sue is hearing! As she likes to say, "WWHT." (Who Would Have Thought)

As we become skilled at reframing, we will become more able to discern between thoughts and actions that are disempowering and those that are empowering. We will be able to "take the best, and change the rest."

Just imagine what would happen if reframing took over as a form of positive communication? I do believe that we would Hear Lots of Applause!

Okay—just for practice—try your hand at reframing:

"I never get anything right!"

_____

"Would you stop that awful whining?"

_____

What phrase would you use that will help you express what you want to happen?

_____

_____

What funny or unusual word or phrase could you use with someone in your family or workplace that would help defuse an uncomfortable situation?

_____

_____

What secret code or signal could you use to help someone be more comfortable with a situation?

_____

_____

Please share with me how any of these communication opportunities helped you hear applause or helped someone else hear applause?

_____

_____

"How Bad Do You Want It" by Tim McGraw

Submitted by Lyndon Blakesley, Sydney, Australia and

Milton, Massachusetts

"I have big dreams. And I want them to happen. I am the first one in my family to not only graduate from college, but to also get my CPA license, and I'm half way through a masters degree in accounting. I did this in the USA, in Massachusetts. I have been fortunate to have wonderful people help me along the way, but I know that it ultimately is up to me if I want my dreams to happen. The music to this song kind of revs me up and puts me in the driver's seat for action!"

Lyndon is a CPA for a multinational
financial services company.

"Right Now" by Van Halen

Submitted by Tabitha Scholtz Jowett,
Pleasant Garden, North Carolina

"The message is simple: 'What are you waiting for?' When I hear 'Right Now', I am reminded to let go of the past, plan for the future, live and work for the moment. Entrepreneurs must be self-motivated to excel; Van Halen reminds me that only action can produce results. Action always overcomes fear. Don't let it stand in your way!"

Tabitha is the Triad Regional Account manager
with America's Best Companies.

Learn more at: www.GoWithABC.com/Tabitha
and/or SmallBizSuccess@triad.rr.com

Action and Action Words

Nothing speaks louder than action, and action speaks louder than words. Put the right positive actions and the right action words together and you can have some serious positive *mojo* happening!

Also, nothing speaks louder than non-action and non-action speaks louder than words.

We believe what people are *doing* over what they are saying. Ideas, plans, and talk all are fine as starting points, but nothing is going to happen without action. Leaders are not afraid of action— well thought-out action. Not action just for the sake of action or notoriety, but action with a purpose. You want to be successful enough to make things happen! Napoleon Hill reminds us: "The world has a habit of making room for the man whose words and actions show that he knows where he is going."

This does not mean you can't have fun and be spontaneous, and everything must be planned out. It simply means that when you are planning something that will impact your life, time, energy or family, such as joining an organization, think of your purpose for joining this particular organization, how you are going to be an active participant, and why.

Action is how people see you as proactive, how you prepare yourself, how you plan, and how and when you get things done.

It demonstrates how you handle different situations. Companies, businesses, schools, and internships are looking for doers. They want people who will participate and add to the overall well-being of the organization. They want people who aspire to success and demonstrate results.

Here's a paradigm shift:

Don't sell yourself short. Show people that you are worth working with and are worth the investment. One effective way to let others know this is by interspersing action words in your communication. The action words have more power when backed up with specific examples. Action words help people visualize more clearly the activity you led, did, or participated in. This is not bragging. This is showing your personal power and that you've invested in yourself. It shows that you care and are willing to go the extra mile by being more specific about what you do and who you are. It shows you pay attention to details and respect their time and position. It is what can differentiate you from the others, making you stand out from the crowd.

As you can see, we are talking **communication** here. We are talking about building relationships that will make a significant difference in you life and in the lives of others. You are going to show that you care by asking questions. You are going to shift your attitude and be more focused on being *more interested* than being *interesting*. You need to remember that it is really about others, too, not just yourself.

Five Ws

Use the **Five Ws** – Who, What, When, Where, Why (represented by your fingers), and the **H -** How (your palm), and the **R -** Results (feeling that internal applause), as a systematic way of putting your action words and thoughts in a coherent form. I like to call this my Helping Hand Mnemonic Device or memory aid. It is a natural way you can use when networking or learning about someone after the introductions are over.

The Five W's, the H, and the R can also be "handy" memory boosters when trying to remember what you are attempting to share. It can add a natural flow to the conversation when interspersed with connecting words or phrases like, "I remember you saying…" "Tell me more…" "That must have been…"

They can also help you in decision-making since they help you become more specific in your thought-process. It's like a GPS (Global Positioning System) positioning you to getting the most out of your communication skills. It is communication in the palm of your hand!

By doing this, you actually get a better sense of self, of accomplishment, and that will give you the confidence you need to put your best foot forward and encourage others to do the same. Let's give it a try with some examples:

Who: Who are you? Who do you work for? Who do you know at this event? Who did you come with? Who invited you? Who is someone that helped you in your career? Who is/was your mentor? Who do you mentor? Who made a difference in …? Who do you partner with for…?

What: What type of work interests you? What type of work do you do? What motivated you to open your business? What motivates you to stay in your business? What sports do you like? What sports do participate in? What are your favorite kinds of movies, books, pets, etc.? What part of town do you live in? What church or organizations do you belong to?

When: When did you get here? When did you find out about this meeting, event, or class? When are you going on vacation this year? When did you move to (city)? When are you planning to join…? When are you going to make those exciting changes in your business?

Where: Where were you born? Where are you planning your next event? Where does your family live now? Where do your children go to school? Where is your favorite restaurant? Where do you get the best return on your investment for…?

Why: Why did you choose this school, meeting, city, church, movie, or play? Why did you move here? Why did you get that (animal) for a pet? Why did you choose the career path you did? Why did you choose to open the type of business you have?

How: How did you hear about this event, concert, park, or restaurant? How did you break your arm? How did you do on the interview? How prepared do you think you were? How did you prepare yourself for your job/occupation/business?

Results: Do you think you passed the test? Do you think the chances are good for you to get that job? Did your team win? Did you meet a lot of new people? What kind of results are you planning to achieve this year in your business? If you make the changes you just told me about, what results are you expecting that would be different from last year at this time?

There are so many more questions that can be added to each category, but at least these are a start and will give you some confidence as you add to your repertoire of questions and comments. As you practice these before hand, you will become more and more comfortable and self-assured in social situations.

One of my colleagues, Joan Calvert, has business matchmaking down to an art. She is a remarkable, generous, and humble person. Her thoughtfulness and professionalism shine through on a daily basis. She genuinely wants people to be successful and she will do everything in her power to help in any way that she can. She effectively uses the five Ws and the H questions, but then she goes even further.

"I've so enjoyed learning all these things about you. Now, how can I help you with…?" She not only asks this question, she will take that person to meet the person that could make it happen or she will even drive that person herself to meet the people that could possibly make it happen. From her vast network of contacts, she sees connections others might miss, and she's quick to make the needed introduction. Talk about being action-oriented! You only need to watch her and listen to her to learn how to be truly effective. She turns *networking* into *net-**worth**-ing!* This is a person who is true to her word. Joan is a person who truly sees the person and not just a sale or prospect. Now you might not think that this is any big deal; however, to those people just starting out in a new community or a new business this can make a huge impact on the future of their success. She makes a difference in your world.

Joan enjoys sharing her philosophy for success in business "networthing." Let's listen...

Joan Calvert

"Sitting around the family dinner table I learned at an early age the value and art of fellowship. My family gave me an acute awareness of the appreciation for developing relationships that has guided me throughout my career and led me to the various roles that I now serve within the community. I also learned that if you do things from the heart, and do things willingly and with love, you don't have any worries. I have come to realize that we all need some form of support system no matter what we do or where we are in our lives.

"I began my career with Pepsi-Cola Company and ITT World Directories in Manhattan. My early introduction to Greensboro, North Carolina, was in the early Seventies when my husband, Cal, and I came south. We were affected by a management downsizing at Pepsi Cola and an opportunity to join Lorillard Tobacco Company. Home was New York and of all things, New York City. The city that never sleeps! Imagine tall skyscrapers, endless shopping, fine restaurants, the theater, and more importantly, and unknown to me at the time, the perfect training ground for what was yet to come. All this helped tremendously as I faced new challenges in a city that was growing and the benefits that southern hospitality and fellowship would create! I recognized that my first step was to build strong relationships, both professionally and socially. I did not want to be known as "a damn Yankee." I wanted to become an integral part of my new city. I wanted to add value.

"This first taste of business in the South became my passion. I learned how to make time for what's important, and in doing so, I stepped up to chair a myriad of committees and worked tirelessly on projects of personal and civic interest.

"Cal passed away ten years ago, yet I have no plans of returning to New York. This has become my home. My connections keep me firmly rooted to the Triad. When I lost my husband, I learned that sometimes in life a farewell ending often ushers in a new beginning. My family, friends, and coworkers have provided a supportive, comfortable environment to make me look and feel better.

"It is important to note that there will always be challenges to overcome, but time and opportunity to build relationships will transition any obstacles into opportunities. Ken Canion once said, 'Ability means nothing without visibility. We must learn how to influence, persuade, and condition others.'

"To me, connecting and meeting people is the easy part. Connections open opportunities. I attend breakfast events and after hours events; I participate in meetings and networking groups. But my true concern is to follow up and follow through. Little things can make a big difference. Do you remember names? Do you listen to the conversation and remember something about the person the next time you meet? Do you make them feel special and show you care? Do you make strategic introductions to others in their sphere of influence?

"It was a cold day in New York way back when, yet I remember four quotes my boss, soon to become my husband, said:

- Actions speak louder than words.

- When interacting with people, roll out the red carpet.

- Good habits never go out of style.

- Enthusiasm is contagious.

"I believe that he and I practiced this for 33 years of marriage. Marriage counselors...take heed...

"I have learned that one of the greatest secrets is to be a giver. Most people just laugh when they hear that the secret to success is giving. Then again, most people are nowhere near as successful as they wish they were.

"Just remember that we can all develop the skills that can make us all great connectors. Go for it!"

WOW! Thanks, Joan! I think she's definitely earned a round of applause—plus!

In times of doubt, you can build up your self-worth by going back and reviewing things that you actually did and the positive results that were achieved by your actions. I like to call these *affirmations on steroids*! Be sure that you include the all-important and appropriate action words as part of these self-reviews. Write them down. Why not keep them in a folder so they are all together when you need a personal or emotional boost? You could even simply save them in a special file in your computer.

Action Words

To get you started, here is a list of some action words that I've found in the dictionary. You can certainly add more action words as you become more pro-active in your undertakings.

...accelerate, achieve, acquire, activate, adapt, add, adjust, adopt, advance, advertise, advise, aide, allocate, analyze, anticipate, apply, appoint, approve, arrange, assess, assign, attain, attract, audit, author, authorize, balance, broaden, build, calculate, chair, champion, change, chart, choose, clarify, classify, collaborate, compile, conduct, consolidate, construct, consult, contribute, convert, coordinate, create, critique, define, delegate, demonstrate, design, determine, develop, edit, employ,

enable, encourage, enforce, engage, enhance, enlist, establish, evaluate, examine, expand, expedite, facilitate, finance, find, focus, forecast, formalize, form, furnish, gather, generate, grant, guide, handle, head, hire, host, identify, implement, improve, increase, influence, inform, initiate, inspect, install, instruct, integrate, interpret, interview, introduce, invent, lead, locate, maintain, manage, market, maximize, measure, mediate, mentor, modernize, monitor, motivate, negotiate, nurture, obtain, opened, operate, orchestrate, order, organize, outline, overhaul, oversee, perfect, perform, persuade, pioneer, plan, position, prepare, present, preside, prevent, publicize, publish, pursue, qualify, quantify, raise, recommend, recruit, redesign, reduce, refine, reinforce, remedy, remodel, renew, reorganize, repair, replace, report, represent, request, research, resolve, restore, restructure, revamp, reveal, reverse, review, revise, revitalize, reward, save, schedule, screen, secure, select, separate, serve, shape, shorten, simplify, sell, solve, spearhead, specify, speak, spur, stabilize, staff, stimulate, streamline, strengthen, structure, study, submit, suggest, summarize, supervise, supply, support, surpass, survey, synchronize, tailor, target, teach, test, train, transfer, translate, transmit, travel, triple, unite, upgrade, utilize, validate, verify, view, vitalize, witness, win, write...

Have you noticed how, after these words, there could be a how, or when, or a by, that is *understood*? I like to think of these action words as *open words*. They allow the speaker, writer, and listener to begin thinking of what comes after, thinking how the action was completed or is to be completed and allows for more discussion. When the right words are in place, one can garner the necessary momentum to make things happen. Take the time to prepare your presentations, speeches or sessions so that the words chosen have optimal impact. It makes a difference when the correct words or phrases are used; people are more apt to sit up and pay attention and will even be more willing to participate if needed. The right action words or phrases are invaluable. Think about what a difference this would make in your sales.

Ask the writer to use action words when requesting or writing a letter of recommendation and please, use them yourself when asked to write a letter of recommendation for someone.

The Dreaded "Elevator Speech"

Let's face it. The fact is...everyone is in sales. We want people to like what they see in us. Whatever area you work in, you do have clients and you do need to sell—not only your product, but you. Since you are always on display and selling your expertise, ideas, product, personality, etc., you must always be prepared to put your best foot forward, not only when you are saying your elevator speech. There is always someone watching you, whether you know it or like it. What type of person are you selling? What is it that people are seeing, witnessing, making decisions about?

Most of us find preparing and saying an elevator speech— that all important 30–60 second commercial, to be a daunting task to undertake as well as memorize. Yet, if you are proud and comfortable with the person you have been "selling", and you use action words, the message becomes easier to construct and share, and chances are, the message will be much more effective and will have more credibility. Begin with action. Avoid beginning with telling about yourself. This is a subtle way of "bragging"

For example:

"The desired effect was achieved! Our chemist took a sample to check for soil composition that might have led to the erosion. Our landscape architects assessed the damage from the erosion, terraced the slope in the front of our customer's house so that their flowers and shrubs really complemented the existing landscape. They managed to do this during the weekend while the owners were at home so that any questions or challenges could be taken care of immediately. We have since received three referrals from these clients."

Or:

"Wow! The shores of Buffalo Creek surely did look cleaner! The members of the Ecology Club collected one hundred and fifty bags of trash from Buffalo Creek. I coordinated this event, encouraged a little healthy competition by motivating the teams with prizes that were donated by local business owners, and then reminded our members about the benefits of thanking the business owners and our sponsors. What an awesome day!"

Action words do make a difference!

I challenge you to write a 45-second elevator speech about you, your work, your company, or your school. Don't forget the action words!

_____

_____

_____

_____

_____

_____

_____

_____

_____

_____

Dare to be selective on your chosen words. Dust off that thesaurus or learn how to use the on-line thesaurus. Check on synonyms to be sure that the word you have chosen is truly the word that is best suited for your thought process or activity. Say what you mean and mean what you say. Take the time necessary to do it the right way. Paying attention to the details is very important and can make a difference in whether you Hear Applause or not!

Do you think using action words allows one to be more specific? Why?

_____

_____

_____

Which action words would you appreciate someone using when writing a letter of recommendation for you? Why?

_____

_____

_____

Are there any other action words that could more specifically help you that are not on this list?

_____

_____

_____

Please share with me how having an elevator speech containing action words would most likely have you hearing applause?

_____

_____

_____

"You Can Get It If You Really Want" by Jimmy Cliff

Submitted by Kathy Bowman Atkins,
High Point, North Carolina

"It has been my experience in life that being the smartest or being lucky or having great wealth is not the key to getting what one really wants—what's really important to them. I believe it's about having the will and determination to continue to strive for what one wants, with a positive attitude. Against almost all other odds and obstacles I have seen people achieve great things with a positive attitude and the willingness to work hard and take some risks. In my own life I try to remember this when I start to get a 'defeatist' attitude."

Kathy is the President and co-founder of The Lattitude Group—a firm specializing in Strategic Business Planning and Leadership/Management Development. Since 2002, The Lattitude Group has delivered results for more than 160 clients in 20+ industries throughout the U.S. and Canada in the for-profit and non-profit sectors.

Learn more at: www.lattitudegroup.com
and/or kathy@tlgrp.com

"Fly By Night" by Rush

Submitted by Holly La Perriere, Newport News, VA

"This song for me, is about the courage to change… whether it is to have the courage to change something that isn't working in your life, or deciding to dive into a new career path…or to continue to grow and change your life yet again for the possibility of new adventures and, more importantly, having the guts to take that first step."

Holly is a Clinical Research Coordinator at Health Research of Hampton Roads.

Perception—Do You See What I See?!

Perception is how we perceive things, people, and situations. It is said that perception is reality. It doesn't matter what reality is. What matters and makes a difference is your perception of that reality, what you believe. Dr. Wayne Dwyer said that, "When you change the way you look at things, the things you look at change." One of the challenges that many of us face each day is to have a positive perception of ourselves. Perhaps we still equate a positive perception of ourselves to having an inflated ego or being conceited.

So we need a paradigm shift. We need to work on our self-limitations and get on with it. Are you up to the challenge? Do you think you are worth it? Are you now starting to understand the power of YOU? Good!

Get Off My "But"

How often are you setting yourself up for defeat instead of success? It's quitting even before you've tried. Do you hear yourself saying things like, "Well, you know…**but**, computers are not one of my strong points."

Or "**But**, I'm not a business or corporate person."

Or "**But**, it's been so long since I've been in school."

Or "**But**, I've never been a good writer."

Or "**But**, do I really have time to do this?"

OR any other "**buts**" like that.

I found myself saying things like that. It was up to me to turn those self-limiting thoughts into positive ones and take action on them.

It was time to **GET OFF MY BUT**! No more excuses! No more whining! If I wanted to be successful in this day and age and really achieve some of my dreams and goals, I had to change my perception on how I viewed myself and did things.

Let me to share some of the steps I took to get me "off my but"…

But…Computers are not among my strong points. Technology is a major force in today's business world, as well as in many people's personal lives. This area scared the weebie-jeebies out of me! I was still scarred from a computer course I took when I was teaching in New Jersey. I had enrolled in a summer course on how computers could enhance my classroom teaching. The principal of our school and the superintendent of our school district were also in this class! I thought I was coming along just fine until…Oh no!!! Where did my lesson plan on *The Planets and the Solar System* that I worked so hard on go?! Try as hard as he could, even the computer teacher could not figure out where it went! Luckily, I had attended all the classes and everyone there had witnessed my work in progress. They all agreed that I was a good candidate for at least an A in this class. To this day, that lesson plan is still somewhere in cyberspace!

Action: I've since taken several computer classes and my confidence and expertise have improved tremendously. I've also had some people tutor me in specific areas. Now I am not only more literate in computer technology, but I participate in social-networking sites, offer teleseminars, teleconferences, webinars, and online courses. You *can* overcome the challenges of technology!

But…I've never been in business or corporate before. I was a teacher for twenty-three years, and I had a captive audience. Students came to me, willingly or not so willingly. There was no cold calling; I did not have to find customers or clients.

Action: Again, there are classes, networking groups, and business organizations that were more than happy to get me started and they still support my endeavors. Today I am a successful personal coach for college students and president of LATTITUDE 4 U. I also have my own publishing company, Applause Publishers.

But…Should I go for my master's degree or not…It's been sooo long! Oh no—will I have to take my GREs again?

Action: I did some research and found the perfect program for my situation. The University of North Carolina at Greensboro (UNCG) offers a Master of Arts in Liberal Studies (MALS) Degree Program that is a perfect fit for my new career. Wow! Just think of all the experiences I can bring to the discussions and what I can learn from the diverse groups of people attending these classes. I could even have a focus on Leadership, which is major part of what I offer my clients. So I thought, "I'll never know until I try." By the way, I proudly graduated in December 2008!

But…Writing? No way… until now, oh my! All through elementary, junior high, and high school, I could swear that my language arts and writing teachers cut open a vein when they edited my writing assignments. There was so much red on my papers!

Action: Find programs and tutors that will guide me and encourage me in this area. And…practice, practice, practice. Now I welcome these red marks, or marks of any color, because no one is perfect! Another action I took as a language arts teacher was never to use a red pen for editing.

But...Do I really have time to do this? Will I be able to manage my time well enough so that I can fit all of these new goals into my already busy schedule?

Action: Come to grips with the notion that there is no time management. Time management is really self-management. Everyone has the same amount of time; it is equally allotted to all of us. There is no *time* to manage. Time is time. How I choose to manage myself in accordance to the 24 hours in a day is up to me. If I was to have people perceive me as successful, they needed to see that I valued myself as to what time meant to me, if I used it wisely, and did not take it for granted. This was a big *paradigm shift* for me to deal with. It kind of took the wind out of my sails and was now something else I couldn't complain about. If it was to be, it was going to be up to me to make the right use of my time. I needed to do a time inventory. I needed to think about the ways I *did* use my time. This was a commodity that could not be wasted if I was to achieve the dreams I had in mind. Oh yes, I found that it was perfectly acceptable to delegate to others the tasks and responsibilities that that I was not so proficient in or simply did not like to do (and that made me cranky and ineffective).

Harvey McKay keeps me in line with his words of wisdom: "Time is free, but it is priceless. You can't own it, but you can use it. You can't keep it, but you can spend it. Once you've lost it, you can never get it back."

I found that when I shared my challenges and solutions with others, it gave me more credibility because I rose to the occasion, developed the necessary skills, was persistent and patient, and began to reach some of my goals and dreams. Much to my surprise, I found that most people were willing and able to work with me. People gravitate towards leaders and people who are successful and really want to be a part of this.

There is no room for "But I can't..." in today's world if you are planning to get ahead and make things happen, if you truly want to make that dream or goal a reality. There is plenty of room, though, for using the *Helping Hand* to promote action, the *Helping*

Hand of the 5 Ws, the H and the R from the *Action* Chapter: When will I? What do I need to do? Who can help me? When will it happen? Where do I need to go to make it happen? How can I... to get the results that I want and deserve?

Uh-huh! You **do** get the picture. You can't get to the top by sitting on your "but." No more excuses!

I Have a Question...

Another area that needs attention for many people is the image they project when asking questions. I was recently at a conference and could not help but notice how the questions to the presenter were phrased. For instance: "I'm sorry, but I am so confused about what you just said. Would you please go over that again?" versus "Would you please clarify the three points you just shared with us?" Why do you feel the need to apologize or depreciate yourself when asking a legitimate question?

Another one: "You're going to think this question is so stupid (giggle, giggle)..." versus Simply asking the question in a professional way. Why demean yourself?

I found myself starting to take offense as to how some of the questions were asked. I wished the questions had been stated in a stronger, more positive way. I felt that it reflected on all of us.

The quality of your questions has a direct impact on the quality of the answers you receive. Ask high-quality questions. Practice asking questions so that you will project a positive, powerful, professional image.

Why, Thank You!

We also need to learn how to take compliments graciously. For instance: Someone compliments you on the outstanding job you did presenting at the conference. It **is** OK to thank that person and maybe mention that this is a topic that you enjoy sharing and that you are happy that he was able to get some value out of the presentation. This is not being egotistical, but professional.

By accepting the compliment, you are also acknowledging the professionalism of the person who complimented you.

This also goes with compliments about your clothes, hair, cooking, etc. When you deflect the compliment, you've caused the other person to focus on negative things instead of enjoying and accepting the gift of the compliment. When you do not accept the compliment, it could reflect on the judgment or credibility of the person complimenting you.

Again, it's OK to practice taking compliments graciously.

Really Now...

Other people's perception of you is important to your business and personal success. It is not only what people know about you, but also what they remember about you. What image are you projecting about yourself? Are you a problem solver? Are you action-oriented? Are you a team player? Are you unforgettable?

The first time I met Cindie Brown was as she and her husband, Scott, were going up some pretty steep and winding cement steps to a meeting we were both attending. Someone had mentioned to me that Cindie was blind and I remember being shocked that she was going up these steps proudly and unaided. She was talking and laughing with Scott as he introduced her to me. Her poise and warmth came through and I knew then that she would be a good friend and also have an impact on my life. Boy! I soon found that I had a lot to learn about this unique individual. I was talking with Cindie on the phone as she was making some of her delicious Strawberry Bread for a friend's birthday. She shared her side of the story with me:

Cindie Brown

"I found out early on that I had to teach people how to be around me and let them know that I was really just like them. I was a person. I was not invisible because I was blind. They can talk directly to me; I am able to hear, talk, and communicate. It was hard to be accepted and I did go through a lot of cruelty especially when I was young.

"I thought of my blindness not so much as a handicap but as a darn nuisance. I had to continually ask for help, and I needed to accept help. I was fiercely independent and was determined not to be left out. I wanted to be like other kids—or bust! I had the coolest mom for a blind girl. She encouraged me to experience as many things as I wanted to, within certain limits, of course. When dad realized that I wouldn't break and that I was determined, in his quiet way he enthusiastically joined mom in my learning experiences. I learned how to ride a bike, swim, roller-skate, climb trees, water ski, and surf (that was *not* cool!). I was permitted to try so many things! We went on many family trips and my family all made sure that I got to 'feel' what they would see.

"I found that there were so many more things that I could do than couldn't do. I made up my mind that this was the way my life would be, and that I was going to make it work for me and those around me. I was not ever going to quit. I was going to be successful. People were going to enjoy being around me.

"I was blessed with an above average intelligence and did quite well in school. At times I felt a little socially inept, but I didn't let that stand in my way. At age twenty-one, when I was in college, I had the opportunity to study in Germany for two semesters—alone. Now that was an experience! I did learn to speak German and that helped a lot. I not only graduated from college, but I also have earned a Masters Degree.

"My husband, Scott, is a blessing. We have such a cool relationship. We do so many things together. He constantly challenges and encourages me to stretch myself. It's a blessing to be included in so many things that my family and friends do. I am part of a normal, wonderful, fun, and active family. We camp, hike, snow ski, go to sporting events together. I even was asked to sing the national anthem at one of my son's wrestling events!

"Life is good, as good as I ever hoped it could be. I have so many people to be thankful for. I do believe that my strong faith has helped me overcome many of my challenges. I do believe that you can be and do whatever you perceive yourself to be and do. And when people see you as a successful person, then that is quite an achievement."

Thank you, Cindie, for sharing your story with us. Hopefully you will change people's perception of all the things a "handi-capped" person can do if they have the courage and support to achieve their dreams. You never cease to amaze me. You certainly deserve a round of applause!

Perception is really important—at school, at home, or at place of work. I will take a school example first. I can remember one year when I was teaching that we had an especially difficult group of seventh-graders. They had always been perceived as "bad" and challenging, and they sort of took some pride in this label. Parents were used to getting phone calls on what their children were doing wrong on whatever day. It's almost as if the problem was just getting too out of hand, and people didn't quite know what to do about it. Of course, the students were not doing as well as they could in school, either. What could we, as teachers, do? We certainly did not want to go through a whole school year like this!

We decided that, several times a week, we would call parents from each of the two seventh-grade classes. This was to be a friendly call sharing something positive about the child. It was interesting: when the parent answered the phone and when they realized it was "The Teacher," one could feel the unease and embarrassment even before the conversation started. The parent was expecting bad news, and instead was surprised with good news about their child. One could feel the surprise and happiness through the phone. Most of the time the message was relayed to the child and some type of reward was given. Kids started talking about this at school. They were now being perceived as worthy of good phone calls, and the positive response from home was kind of nice to get; well you get the picture. Kids were anxiously waiting for their parents to get…that… call. No one wanted to be left out from getting a good call to their parent. It became kind of a status symbol. Kids rose to the occasion. They became prouder of themselves. Little by little we saw positive changes happening at school, and parents shared with us the subtle changes happening at home. It wasn't perfect, but the year ended up being quite a good year.

Perception: as the students perceived that they were good and capable of behaving well and getting good grades, they became more successful. They enjoyed hearing the applause.

This same kind of tactic can be employed in any situation. People rise up to what is expected of them, of what it is perceived that they can do.

Enter LaToya Marsh, Special Olympics Cheerleading Coach. She is the 2009 winner of the North Carolina Medallion Award and was Second runner up for the Glamour Magazine Woman of the Year. LaToya is also the reigning Miss Greensboro. She also has a passion for helping others and volunteers for eight different organizations within the Triad, including Special Olympics North Carolina, Multiple Sclerosis Society, American Cancer Society, and Make a Wish, to name a few. Here she is to share her story:

LaToya Marsh

"Thanks, Leona. I owe the successes in my life that you mentioned to all the volunteer work I have done with all my organizations and especially my cheer squad. I love cheerleading! I had been a cheerleader for thirteen years and had been a Special Olympics volunteer before I asked Charyl Clark, the Greensboro director, about starting a cheerleading team. Why not work with some of these girls and help them towards a dream? I would be pairing my love of cheerleading with a hands-on role in making the difference in others lives. It would require taking a class on challenges and physical limitations and what could aggravate their conditions. Seven girls signed and this was the start of the Greensboro Diamonds.

"It was a first-year squad of teenage and young adult cheerleaders with mental or physical disabilities. Coaching and mentoring these girls was a role that I found to be very rewarding. Initially I thought it might be difficult, but from the first moment I met the girls on the team, I fell in love with it. I looked forward to practice every week and I just loved seeing how happy it made each of them to know they were cheerleaders. They never once gave up or said, 'I can't do this.' One of the girls left me in tears. She said that she was not one of the popular girls and never thought that she could cheer. I made it my mission to teach them that they had to believe in their abilities and in themselves. I created cheers and elements that were good for the girls. Our squad has a variety of abilities, and I wanted to take their strengths and mesh them together. I believed in them and they knew it. We made a really strong squad. The joy my cheerleaders bring to spectators is surpassed only by the joy the team gets from performing.

"While I enjoyed my role as a mentor, I learned just as much from these athletes. I credit them for teaching me to look at life differently. I came to realize how silly it is to get upset over the little things. When I see what these athletes overcome everyday, it really puts things in perspective.

"This experience has been so positive. I am already excited about the next season. I plan to have my squad performing at halftime of a game at each of the Greensboro/High Point colleges. Go team!"

This very special squad earned a gold medal at an area competition and then a bronze medal at the 2009 SONC Basketball &Cheerleading Tournament. It was a fantastic season and the accolades are still coming. LaToya makes sure that these girls have a different perception of themselves and encourages others to have a different perception of them, too. Please join me in giving LaToya and her squad a warm round of applause.

If you are interested in learning more about the Special Olympics, please visit: www.specialolympics.org. You will also notice that the states that participate in Special Olympics will have their own sites.

Carpe Diem! Seize the Day and you **will** Hear Applause!

What excuses do you need to stop using so that you can get off your BUT and achieve something important to you?

_____

_____

_____

What is it that you need to do to propel yourself to the successes you endeavor? Are you willing to stretch yourself? How can/will you do this?

_____

_____

_____

What are your biggest time wasters?

_____

_____

_____

What are your biggest distractions? How can you get back on track?

_____

_____

_____

What can you delegate to others so that you can become more efficient in what you need to accomplish?

_____

_____

_____

Please share what you do to give people a good perception of you?

_____

_____

_____

"Fame" by Irene Cara

Submitted by Karen Andriano, Greensboro, North Carolina

"I chose 'Fame' because when I hear this song, I am encouraged to be successful, to work diligently towards my dreams. I am always open to new ideas. I want to make a difference in people's lives!"

Karen is, first and foremost a mother that loves 'unconditionally', a wise Nana, and a true friend to many. By trade she is a Business Administrative professional that uses her life's experiences to making a 'positive difference' to all she encounters."

Learn more at: kandrianos@gmail.com

"Don't Stop Believing" by Journey

Submitted by Linda Blumenfeld, Wilmington and Greensboro, North Carolina

"This has been a favorite song of my husband, Larry, and me since way back in college…and it's a favorite of our family, too. When things are not going quite the way you want them to, think about your strengths and believe in yourself and you can accomplish anything."

Linda is the owner of LBL Marketing, Inc. – perfect for the small business that is seeking affordable marketing solutions with a "big business" feel. The company's focus is connecting the business owner's product or services to its target audience and client.

Learn more at: opbylinda@aol.com

Positive Self-Talk AKA: Affirmations

As your positive self-image grows, so will your ability to achieve your goals and dreams. How you think about, write about or state these goals and dreams is half the battle. Let's work on this.

Positive thinking works! Positive self-talk is a wonderful habit to develop and helps us as we discover our hidden talents. By putting things in positive terms, you open up possibilities. You become a positive thinker, looking for solutions. You are empowered. This is a desired success and leadership skill that will serve you well in your personal and professional lives.

Positive self-talk is also known as **affirmations**, positive statements that we repeat to ourselves on a daily basis or when we need to give ourselves some encouragement or perspective. Using affirmations is a conscious process. Each time you tell yourself something positive, you are reinforcing that you are a wonderful human being and that you are contributing something positive to society; you are reinforcing the positive elements of the affirmation. The more you reinforce this feeling on a conscious level, then the more the subconscious begins to pick up on it. Perhaps you are thinking that this sounds like subliminal messaging. That's OK. You find that little by little you begin to have more faith in yourself and in your skills and talents. It helps develop your sense of personal power.

Affirmations are short, concise, positive statements that you repeat to yourself as often as needed to help you reprogram your mind, while focusing on the positives in your life. Aahh! The power of repetition! Affirmations are very basic tools for success, of self-management, through the intentional choice of thoughts and words and actions. An intentional choice of words can make a world of difference in how your message is relayed and understood.

Positive affirmation statements allow us to strengthen our new attitudes and new habits of thoughts by changing our mental patterns. Affirmations should be included in your goal-setting and achieving process. Affirmations come from within. Learning to use affirmations is a vital tool that will build self-esteem and encourage you to be self-accepting. Affirmations help you focus on your strengths as you are honing your personal development skills. They help you look at the positive aspects of a problem and find appropriate solutions to get you to your desired results.

Some of you might be put off by this concept thinking that it might be too "new-age" for you, but it is a tried-and-true success skill. The power of affirmations can best be recognized when we realize that the mind does not know the difference between real and imagined. For example: It is late at night and you are alone in your house. You heard some noise outside and now you imagine that there might be someone sneaking around outside your house. Are you any less afraid than if you knew for sure that there really was someone out there? Probably not. You are afraid because you imagine a fearful situation.

The use of affirmations to build confidence applies to the same principle, but with a positive goal in mind. We are sort of tricking our mind into visualizing and believing the positive result we are striving for. We are becoming our own cheerleaders.

Witt Chapman is a young man that I've been coaching for a few years. We started working together when he was a sophomore in college at the University of North Carolina School of the Arts. He had decided that he wanted to broaden his horizons and attend a university or music school in Los Angeles or New York that would fulfill the type of music background he wanted to develop. It was the month of April, and he was hoping to get into a new school for the fall semester. Yes, you are thinking… right! Is he crazy?!? That was only a few months away. Could this possibly be done?! We diligently reviewed his reasons, his school records, his work records, his strengths, his weaknesses, possible scholarship applications, grant applications, work-study opportunities. We honed his communication skills so that he could present a polished proposal to his parents and his school so that they would approve this decision. Talk about a major affirmations boost! We pulled out all the plugs. Affirmations and visualizations and hard work kept him focused and on track. And, YES! He *was* accepted at Loyola Marymount University in Los Angeles, his first choice—and not only in the School of Film and Television, but also in the School of Communications and Fine Arts—as a student obtaining dual degrees.

Many of us don't even realize that we are using a form of affirmations when we post quotes that mean something to us, that we find to be inspiring or encouraging. If you can get a handle on this success skill, your perception of reality will change and you will be in more control of your success.

Guidelines

Here are some guidelines for stating affirmations:

- Affirmations should be positive.

- Affirmations should be in the first-person singular and in the present tense.

- Affirmations should be within the realm of your capacity to believe—realistically high.

- Affirmations should be directly related to your goals. You want a certain outcome as a result of repeating the affirmation.

Here are some samples of simple affirmations:

- I communicate well with others.

- I enjoy being prepared.

- I am an empathetic manager.

- I can learn anything I set my mind to.

- I always do my best.

- I use my goals to guide my daily tasks.

- I am a good problem-solver.

- I enjoy being on time. (Not: I hate being late.)

- I treat people with respect and dignity. (Not: I don't gossip.)

- I respect my body. (Not: I don't do drugs.)

- I am a responsible shopper. (Not: I don't shoplift.)

Some people have found that they enjoy being even more specific with their affirmations. They might include feeling words that add positive emotion and depth to their affirmations. They might be even more specific about what they want, rather than being vague. Some might want to focus with a mini-goal in mind. As you use your own affirmations, you might realize that they might not be all completely true; however, these are the skills that you are in the *process of developing*. It is not to say that negative thoughts or self-doubt might not creep into your new self-development, especially if you are prone to low self-esteem. For an affirmation to work, you need to believe that these affirmations *are possible for you.*

Affirmations set the tone for success and allow the brain to process positive actions that need to happen for you to reach your goals.

Lisa Freeman is a friend and colleague who exemplifies how positive self-talk can get you from one job to another. We have been discussing how realizing and developing your talents is very important in your quest to be successful. Lisa always looks at the silver lining in the cloud. When I first met Lisa, she was working for a graphic arts company. Then she needed to find something else and found herself working with a staffing agency. Downsizing occurred several other times with other companies and this forced Lisa to experience several career transitions. Her firm belief in herself and the value of experience keeps her going forward. Well, I'll let Lisa explain all this:

David & Lisa Freeman

"I have always seen myself as a person who likes to see the best in everything. In fact, I have found myself believing this many times when everyone else is ready to give up and give in. Eighteen years in the printing business and thirteen years in the employment industry gave me a variety of experiences ranging from being a business development manager placing IT professionals and engineers, to developing a career in human resources placing technical professionals. My last position was very demanding and required a lot of travel. Yet, no matter how tough my job was, it was my optimism and belief in me that carried me. Through all these transitions, I needed to take some deep, hard looks at my talents and skills to see which of these would benefit me most as I transitioned from one career to another. At times, it was necessary to improve on these skills or to learn new skills that would keep me competitive in this modern work environment.

"So the question is: What creates that motivation and drives a person to see the best? I truly think each of us has a choice every day to choose our attitude, and other people will react to us accordingly. I was so fortunate to have a mom that showed me how you have to make your own happiness in this world. It is your decision; no one can make that choice for you. She also instilled in me the value of who I am and when things got tough, she made sure to affirm me and made sure that I affirmed myself. This has driven me to be the best that I can be at what I do, and to reach out to others in service and to give back by working with several nonprofit organizations. Giving back will change you! Affirming the good in others and helping them acknowledge their gifts and strengths will give you permission to do the same for yourself. If you don't believe in yourself, how can you convince others to believe in themselves?

"My husband, David, and I are both facing other crossroads in our professional careers. We are both now doing things we never would have dreamed we would be doing. David is a professional builder and he has experienced a tremendous hit from these economic times. I have been with Shaklee for a number of years. However, I have now made the decision to build the kind of career in Shaklee where I can leverage all the experience I have gained in past careers and do what I love—develop and build relationships and create change.

"My husband really enjoys cooking and has developed a roasted red pepper cheese spread that everyone raves about. In the midst of all this change, we are stepping forward in faith in marketing this product. We are working to develop several partnerships with several venues to market this cheese product. This is quite a bit different from being a builder!

"What keeps us moving forward when our paths are uncertain? It is the sense of wanting something new, the determination to do more with our lives, and the ability to believe that anything is possible—these are what drive us.

"So, how many people does it take to create change? If you thought—ONE—you are right! As you face challenges and embrace changes, surround yourself with positive influences and enforce what is good, and soon you will see a way to continue."

Thank you, Lisa, for reminding us about the importance of positive thinking and self-affirmation and affirming others, also. Everyone wins this way! You do deserve a round of applause!

By the way, I did taste David's delicious roasted red pepper cheese spread at a fund-raising event for the Women's Resource Center (Lisa is on the Board of Directors for this nonprofit organization) and it is incredible...yum, yum!

Yada, Yada, Yada...

How many times have you found yourself in a situation or group of people where all you hear are negative things? It seems that some people can never find a positive thing to say about anything or anyone. First thing you know, you are adding to the negative tone and heading down a negative spiral yourself. This is a very easy trap to fall into. Those negative vibes will get you nowhere fast. Negative energy is draining. One way that you can deal with this type of situation is, first of all, to be aware of it, and then, choose to make a conscious effort to change it. Be the leader and choose to flip those limiting thoughts and create an affirmation or two. Maybe the affirmations would need to be introduced as questions. If you are in the break room at work, and the discussion is leaning towards gossip or saying negative things about people, bring up something positive and take it from there. Encourage others to start doing the same. Get a positive thinking flow going. This will add more positive energy to the rest of the day, too.

My friend and colleague, Monica Diaz, (www.e-quidam.com/theblog) and the author of *Otheresteem: Regaining the Power to Value Others*, reminds us that we must be aware of the distinction between positive thinking and wishful thinking.

"It is not enough to believe that if only you can think positively enough, that everything will turn out the exact way you think. As popular wisdom states, if you are wishing to win that lottery, you had better go out and buy those numbers!

"Having faith and affirming that the world will conspire with us is not a bad practice. Especially because it will lead you to act with more self-confidence, to move forward with all you've got, to make brave, bold decisions and explore uncharted territories. Positive thinking requires that you act, that you do something to make it happen. You need to affirm yourself. Goals and dreams will not come to fruition by merely thinking about them and wishing about them in positive ways. Just positive thinking will not be sufficient to carry us through to goal achievement. It has to be grounded in realistic analyses of situations, events, skills, etc. Once this is done, we can allow ourselves to move forward and act on our positive thinking. Negative thinking is not necessarily a bad thing. It may cause us to be mindful of whether our thinking moves us forward or holds us back. It may cause us to think twice about something we might want to attempt and therefore be better informed before embarking on a new idea or project. We must always be open to both sides so that we can give equal opportunity to our decisions and goals. This is being realistic and smart."

Saying and using affirmations is like exercise. It must be done regularly and be incorporated into your daily routine. You need to visualize it—feel it—become it. It leads to belief in yourself—and when you truly believe in yourself, good things start to happen.

Using affirmations encourages you to make your thoughts, words, and actions a personal reality. Affirmations are good ways to keep your attitude up and focused. Write your affirmations on your own index cards. Place them in locations where you spend a great deal of time—your office, car, refrigerator door, etc. Carry them with you. We give our clients special little business-card-like holders that can be folded in half and kept in a pocket. Develop a schedule for using them: first thing in the morning, at lunch, before you leave the office, before bed. Aahh! The power of spaced repetition! Consistent efforts at affirmations will convince you that "shift happens!" And when you are shifting into high gear…you will Hear Applause!

One activity I encourage my clients to do is to keep an affirmations or positive thinking journal. A simple black and white notebook will do the trick. Each day my clients are to write down at least three positive things or actions or affirmations that they applied that day. Keeping a written journal of these positive actions is visual proof that you can have control of what you want to accomplish and what you actually did accomplish. They begin to affect your subconscious mind and positively influence your behavior. My clients enjoy sharing these affirmations and positives at our weekly coaching sessions, especially when they start to experience the subtle positive changes in their attitudes and behaviors. Some of the topics that my clients have chosen to include in their "Positives Journal" are: affirmations, small acts of kindness, tapping into their talents, taking the initiative to make positive things happen, thinking about solutions instead of problems, smiling at someone today, what a particular song they heard on the radio meant to them that day, encouraging someone today, motivating you and or someone today, helping someone today, being kind to yourself today, listening to your conscience, choice of language you use, quotes, sayings, songs, stories, articles, comic strips, positive choices they've made, qualities they are developing as they continue on their journey of self-discovery and leadership. Try It! You'll like it!

Let's take affirmations a step further…

Writing and saying affirmations for yourself is certainly a good practice to start and to follow through. Now I challenge you to affirm someone else each day. Find someone to thank, to share the difference that they made in your life or someone else's life, to praise a talent or gift they have that you appreciate, etc. It will keep you in a more positive frame of mind. It may also encourage them to affirm others. You can affirm others by e-mail, snail mail, or phone calls—any way that you can get this affirmation to them. I started doing this a few years ago. The impact it's had on my life as well as on others' lives is amazing. Can you imagine what positive things will come out of something like this?

Another good success habit to develop is to rephrase a statement or thought about yourself in a more positive light. For example:

- I'm curious and I love learning new things (vs. I'm nosy).

- I am reserved and thoughtful (vs. I'm too shy).

- I'm focused and goal-oriented (vs. I work too hard).

- I'm creative (vs. I'm not focused).

- I'm assertive and get things done (vs. I'm aggressive).

- I'm self-assured (vs. I'm vain).

- I'm in control of the situation (vs. I'm bossy).

Again, the intentional choice of words opens the mind to possibilities and helps it to focus on what actions need to be taken to support what you have stated. It focuses the mind in a positive direction, allowing you to be more successful. Using words that have a negative connotation makes us appear negative and not people-friendly or cooperative.

It is well worth the effort to train our minds to think in the positive, to be intentional with our words and thoughts.

One of the elementary schools I taught in encourages its students to say a pledge every morning at the start of their school day. This is a type of daily affirmation that keeps students focused and on task. There is also power in numbers. When a group of people pledge to do their best, there is accountability and a better chance for success. One can feel the power of this group mentality in this pledge:

I am a proud McGaheran Bulldog.

I come to school to learn, and I do learn.

I take responsibility for my behavior and my work.

I show respect for myself and others.

I am doing what I can to make this a great day!

The power of positive words and thoughts is incredible. Using the right words or thoughts is proven to trigger the release of endorphins, which fill you with confidence.

This newfound confidence will help us to envision our success and make it really happen. Happiness comes from within. Affirm that good things will happen and you will Hear Applause!

Now it's your turn to practice writing an affirmation or two:

Think of a way that you might have presented yourself in a less favorable way, and turn it around, using more positive words and phrases.

_____

_____

Please share with me ways that can you affirm someone in your family, at work, or at school. Did you find this activity difficult? If not, why? If so, why?

_____

_____

_____

What were the reactions of the receivers of your affirmations to them? Do these reactions act as a catalyst, encouraging you to make this a part of your success goals?

_____

_____

_____

"Joy to the World" by Three Dog Night

Funmitted by Dan Allen, Fort Myers, Florida

"The words are fun and the tune is very happy and peppy and easy to sing along with. Feels like a celebration. It makes me feel carefree and makes me want to dance and sing. It always puts me in a positive mood."

Dan celebrates life with his family in Fort Myers, Florida. He is also the Director of Club Z! - a tutoring service for students.

Learn more at: www.clubZtutoring.com and/or danallenfm@comcast.net

"Smile" by Uncle Kracker

Submitted by Kristen Leonard, Greensboro, North Carolina

"All you have to do is to listen to this song and it'll have you smiling and laughing. This song just makes you HAPPY! You can't help but look at the bright side of things and be thankful for all you have. It always puts me in a positive mood."

Kristen is a banking officer- a Commercial Banking Specialist at Southern Community Bank and Trust.

Learn more at: www.smallenoughtocare.com and/or kristen.leonard@smallenoughtocare.com

Laughter: One of the 5 Keys to Emotional Intelligence

Live and learn...learn and live...and don't forget to add a healthy dose of laughter to your living and learning! Some words that come to mind when I think of laughter are smiling, giggling, grinning, happiness, surprises, humor, joy, playfulness, sharing, being positive, and friendship. Laughter can put things in perspective. Laughter helps us look at the bright side of things. It helps us look at the positives. It puts the little skip in our step. Laughter can make our soul sing. Laughter is empowering. Laughter adds joy and zest to our lives, improves our moods, eases anxiety and fear, and relieves stress. Laughter strengthens relationships, enhances teamwork, promotes group bonding, helps defuse conflict, and attracts others to us. Laughter...just... makes...you...feel...good! So...what's not to like about laughter? It should play an integral part in our daily living experiences.

I'm not saying that we shouldn't take life seriously. There certainly is a definite need for serious, purposeful work, relationships, plans, etc. Yet sometimes we get so caught up in what we are doing that we take the fun out of it for ourselves and others we are working with, adding stress to our lives.

I love this quote from Reba McEntire, one of my favorite country singers...

"To succeed in life you need three things: a wishbone, a backbone and a funny bone."

In a leadership setting this could mean…

Wishbone: hopes, dreams, goals, achieving

Backbone: strength, perseverance, vision, plan

Funny bone: humor, it should be a necessity in our lives. For goodness sakes…even when we hit our funny bones we get a mixture of pain, sometimes tears, but also laughter—crazy isn't it?

A true positive person doesn't refuse to recognize the negatives, but refuses to dwell on them. Dwelling on negatives is self-limiting. Being happy doesn't mean that everything is perfect. It means that you've decided to look beyond the imperfections and to find the right solutions to get the results you are striving for.

Gordon. B. Hinckley, an American religious leader, says, "Go forward in life with a twinkle in your eye, and a smile on your face, but with a great and strong purpose in your heart."

For those of you who are interested in improving your health, listen up! Yes, there are many health benefits to laughter. This translates to being a better you, better spouse, better employer or employee, better student, and a better friend.

Linda Hamilton, RN, MSN, is a stress management coach and she shares these thoughts on laughter:

"A smile is an inexpensive way to improve your looks. It can make you look years younger. It's a natural face-lift. It gives your cheeks a natural healthy glow. It makes your eyes twinkle. It makes you look more rested, less tired. When smiling or laughing, you will probably find yourself walking straighter and taller, and that makes you look slimmer, too.

"Laughter relieves fatigue and relaxes your body. A good hearty laugh relieves physical tension and stress, leaving your muscles relaxed for up to forty-five minutes afterward. This improves the function of your blood vessels and increases blood flow which can protect you against a heart attack and other cardiovascular problems. It improves the flow of oxygen to the brain. Your batteries are now recharged, allowing you to stay focused and able to accomplish even more!

"Laughter also boosts the immune system by decreasing stress hormones and increasing immune cells and infection-fighting antibodies, thus improving your resistance to disease.

"Being happy and positive is proven to trigger the release of endorphins, the body's natural feel-good chemicals. Endorphins promote an overall sense of well-being, leading to more self-confidence.

"If you're into vitamins—well the best vitamin to take to be a happy person is… B1!

"And for those of us who hate working any more than we have to—research shows that it takes twenty-six muscles to smile and sixty-two muscles to frown. So…why work so hard! Just smile!"

My friend, Angel Guerrero, loves to make people smile and laugh, even when he's working with them on serious things. Whether it's using his background in chemistry and nutrition educating people with his "You Are What You Eat" presentation or watching his customers' frowns turn into smiles as he develops just the right Website for their business, Angel's sunny personality is what everyone appreciates. I'll let Angel give his take on nutrition and computers:

Angel Guerrero

"I was trying to figure out a way to illustrate the power of good nutrition to people, especially teens. I was concerned about their eating habits. Some of these teens seemed so unhappy with their body image. So this is what my presentation consisted of: a pair of pantyhose nylons, a bucket, water, soda, donuts, chips, cookies, a McDonald's Happy Meal, peanut butter cups, fried chicken, chopped apples, scrambled eggs, juice, canned tuna, salad, celery and carrot pieces, etc. I asked for a volunteer to help me. The volunteer's job was to hold up the nylons while I filled them with as assortment of food that is eaten in a typical day. One leg had food that teens/folk usually are known to eat, the other leg had the healthier food. The audience got to see the effect each type of food could have on their body. It does generate a lot of laughter! It is pretty yucky, though! This example is vivid enough to convince people to be more careful about their eating habits. Often enough I bump into people who have witnessed this presentation and they say that it still has an effect on them. Yes, it is a serious subject; however, this is a pleasant way to deal with it.

"As for computers: I love helping people develop Websites that attract the right clients or customers. I love the fact that my company, AS WEB PROS, has helped thousands of businesses capitalize on us creating or refreshing their online presence. The results are that their Website attracts the right clients or customers, removes doubt that theirs is a professional company, allows them to have content management of their Website, creates positive cash flow as they especially have full support from our technical and marketing staff without annoying contracts or being nickel-and-dimed them to death. We make sure we understand their company's goals and their goals and function with those goals in mind. There's nothing better than to see a happy customer, grinning from ear to ear, empowered with the feeling of being in control of their success. By the way, we also offer all this in Spanish. Se Habla Español."

Angel has unique ways of dealing with serious situations and making them much more pleasant to deal with. He deserves a well-earned round of applause!

(There is a video on my website that shows Angel performing this particular presentation. See if it'll make a difference to you, too.)

Happiness comes from inside. Affirm that good things will happen and they will!

"Happiness is when what you think, what you say, and what you do are in harmony." Mahatma Gandhi

When happy, you project optimism and self-confidence, as well as being open to possibilities. This is part of emotional intelligence, helping us strengthen our relationships, succeed at work, and overcome life's challenges.

People are attracted to happy, funny individuals. Laughter draws others to you and keeps them by your side. A positive bond is created when we laugh together. This bond acts as a buffer against stress, disagreements, and disappointments and forms a team mentality.

How many of you would rather be with a happy, optimistic person, one who smiles more than frowns? Laughter is contagious…when we hear it we look where it's coming from, we are drawn to it.

The ability to use laughter, humor and play in your relationships is one of the five key skills of emotional intelligence. These skills can be learned by anyone, at any time. Laughter has been found to be so important for our emotional and physical health that there is even an organization, a company called World Laughter Tour, Inc., that focuses on interpreting promising laughter theories and practices into multi-generational, multi-cultural health and happiness related programs—preventing hardening of the attitudes; providing methods that are uplifting, simple, and powerful; making the world a better place; helping people make better health choices; providing the best value in training; for individuals, organizations, and service to the community. Its grand vision is that together we can lead the world to health, happiness, and peace through laughter. (www.worldlaughtertours.com)

My friend Marilyn Sprague is a Certified Laughter Leader (CLL) affiliated with this company and has her own award-winning training company called Miracles & Magic. Through customized training programs, professional speaking keynotes, and therapeutic laughter programs, she serves as a catalyst for long-term positive change. Marilyn has the gift of touching the hearts of her audience that encourages them to change their behavior and achieve better results...in a happier way. If you ever get an opportunity to experience this type of activity, don't pass it up!

Learn more at: www.miraclesmagicinc.com and/or marilyn@miraclesmagicinc.com

Erinn and Nelson Diaz are the founders of First in Flight Entertainment. Yes! You figured right. They are lucky enough to make having fun and laughter as part of their daily routine. Erinn would like share her background on how what she does is beneficial for businesses, too.

Erinn & Nelson Diaz

"I started my performance career when my parents signed me up for tap dancing lessons when I was three. I kept at it so hard that I started competing when I was very young. It made me so happy when I could make an audience smile! By the time I was six, I had already won my first of what would be eleven national titles in tap dance and I was loving every second of being on stage. When I was seven, I got into singing and acting, and I practically grew up at the theater working on shows and performing shows both onstage and off. I grew up in

Winston-Salem, North Carolina, but moved to Florida when I was eighteen to become a singer and entertainment hostess on both an island resort and a cruise ship. It was a wonderful experience, but the best part of all was that I met my wonderful husband and business partner, Nelson, in the cruise ship offices. When we 'retired' from the cruise lines, we stayed in South Florida, where I performed all sorts of professional theater, and also ran the Theater League of South Florida, an organization that advocates for the arts in South Florida. I also started The Caroling Company with a couple of friends, a company that provides professional singers in Dickensian costumes to private parties and tree-lighting ceremonies. Bringing the holidays alive is truly a one-of-a-kind experience! When we retired from the cruise line in 2006, we realized that cruising is not only for personal pleasure, but that many businesses and companies use cruise ships as a reward for work well done, to keep employees and other people happy, or for seminars, etc. So it was on this premise that we planned to start our own entertainment business. We moved back to Winston-Salem in 2008 to be back with family. Winston-Salem is, after all, called 'The City of the Arts' and we wanted to do our part to really make it so. We got the idea for the company name from North Carolina's 'First in Flight' slogan on its license plate. Now every time you look at a North Carolina license plate, you'll think of our company—First In Flight Entertainment!

"First in Flight Entertainment specializes in providing customized entertainment for all sorts of events. We provide entertainment for public and private occasions, parties, malls, senior centers, school performances, festivals and fairs, and so much more. Some of the entertainment we do includes celebrity look-alikes, characters, bands, string quartets, compact musical shows, soloists, pianists, murder mysteries, mimes, holiday carolers, emcees, and even customized performances. We know fun! We know how to help people de-stress and enjoy themselves.

"Companies of all sizes know the importance of rewarding their employees for work well done, so quality entertainment at office parties and corporate events is essential. We also believe that small businesses are using entertainment to stand out and market their businesses in a crowd of competitors.

"Recently we opened classrooms in two cities in North Carolina where we will offer a variety of theatre performance classes. This will also give our performers a venue to teach their talents as all of our teachers are professional performers. We love our job because we help make people happy on every level—professional, business, and personal. I can't imagine doing anything else in this world that could make me any happier!"

The ability to laugh, play, and have fun with others not only makes life more enjoyable, it also helps when solving problems, connecting with others, and being more creative. People who incorporate humor and play into their daily lives find that it renews them and all of their relationships. Erinn and Nelson deserve a round of applause for doing their share in this department!

Erinn has also written a book, ***Help! I'm On My Own and Don't Know Where to Start: An Essential Guide to Living On Your Own***, by Erinn Dearth. As mentioned in her story, Erinn moved hundreds of miles away from her parents, and, although her parents really did teach her well, she felt that she also learned from experience what I it was like to live on her own. There were many things to remember and learn, so she decided to put it all down in a book to make it easier for other young people starting off on their own. This book will help put a smile on the face of parents and college students or anyone who is on their own for the first time. Check it out!

Many things in life are beyond our control, particularly the behavior of other people. While taking the weight of the world on your shoulders might be admirable, in the long run it's unrealistic, unproductive, unhealthy and egotistical. It's important to keep things in perspective. When in a funk, recall a point in your life when you felt strong, vibrant, and happy. Relive it, conjure up as many details as possible, use as many of your senses as you can to really feel that memory, and act on it. While you're at it, why not make a list of the good things in your life, funny moments in your life, so they will be close at hand when you need an emotional laughter booster.

It is important to remember that laughing WITH people, not AT people, is the rule of thumb—the one that will get the desired results.

Life brings challenges that can get the best of you. When you *become the problem* and take yourself too seriously, it can be hard to think outside the box and find new and/or improved solutions. But when you *play* with the problem, you can often transform it into an opportunity for creative learning. Laughter and humor can interrupt a power struggle, easing tension and allowing people to reconnect and regain perspective. Shared laughter can allow folks to see problems in new ways and find creative solutions.

An unhappy or difficult boss can wreck your day. If you picture what makes your boss smile or laugh, that will help you rethink and set new goals for the company's success. It can also help you deal with serious matters in a more balanced way.

Think: what would put a smile on my face or make me laugh if I succeed in/with this? This can actually help to keep you more focused on your goals.

We are thinking of the rewards and rewards inspire us, help us set goals, keep us focused, ultimately making us happy, smiling, giggling…Hearing Applause!!!

One of the most important tools you'll need is your SMILE. This could be one of your secrets to success. A smile shows friendship, appreciation, trust, good-will and encouragement. A smile can help manage conflict and take the stress out of situations.

So when going for that all-important job interview remember, you're never completely dressed without a smile...and a firm handshake.

Some people grin and bear it. Others smile and change it. Which person would you rather be?

W.C Fields had the right idea when he shared: *"Start every day off with a smile, and get it over with!"*

Let's offer a toast to each other...Live well...Love much... Laugh often!

What two actions can you incorporate in your day take that will make you happier and more productive?

_____

_____

_____

What two actions can you incorporate in your day that will help someone else be happier and more productive?

_____

_____

_____

What problem can you *play* with that could eventually have a *happy ending?*

_____

_____

_____

Please share with me what the problem was and what you did to achieve this goal?

_____

_____

_____

Please share a song that puts you in a happy mood. Why did you pick this song?

_____

_____

_____

"Eye of the Tiger" by Survivor

Submitted by Zac Engle, Greensboro, North Carolina

"This song gives you the urge to succeed when you are facing a challenge. It is simple and primal. The music pulses, raising your adrenaline—daring you to get down to the basics of what it takes to be a leader."

Zac is a Developmental Officer at Guilford College.

Learn more at: engleza@guilford.edu

"I Hope You Dance" by Lee Ann Womack

Submitted by Estelle Leger, Acushnet, Massachusetts

"This song leaves me in awe every time I hear it. It gives examples of life's experiences and states how one can overcome the daunting challenges life can give us. It speaks of disappointments, reconsiderations; one door closes yet another one opens. It speaks of the faith one needs in the challenges ahead as well as the challenges that are placed upon the proverbial student. As you speak of applause, one can also reflect on dancing, portraying both time being real and time being in constant motion. It also has the listeners thinking of both their past as well as hoping to make the future one that reveals that lessons have been learned by reaching the final goal—to be come a better person."

Estelle is a semi-retired medical technologist.

Authority and Power

Leaders are developed, not born. The degree to which you develop your leadership skills depends solely on you and the effort you put forth in creating your own destiny. There could be a lot of discussion about this topic, but really, even if you carry the gene for leadership, it will not get you very far unless you develop this gift. Why am I talking about leadership? Leadership is a very important quality to develop, since "average" will not get you very far in today's world. What does it take to be a leader, to differentiate yourself from others, to create an impact in our global society? Quite a few success strategies have already been covered in this book. However, the proper use of these success strategies is very important as we start to really understand the workings of the bases of societies and our role in them.

Oftentimes people are thrust into a leadership position, or they are willing to step forward and take on a leadership role. Responsibility and accountability are part of the package deal along with the title and the position. I need not remind you that the best leaders are those who serve others and walk with integrity to better the lives of others. It is not about becoming a leader for the sake of power.

Let's start by looking at authority and power. Most people think they are one and the same. Many people don't give it much thought. But there *is* a difference. I like to consult my Leadership

Book, developed by Resource Associates Corporation. The distinction is made very clear in their literature.

Authority

"Leaders are found in positions of authority, and leaders are also found in everyday situations and groups. Leaders can be found in classrooms, gyms, neighborhoods, and homes. Some leaders have authority and some do not. Some leaders with authority seem to have a hard time getting people to listen and/ or getting things done. Some leaders without any authority seem to be able to get more done than those with authority.

"People have **authority** when they possess certain rights granted to them because of the position they hold. Authority may be defined as a right granted to give commands, enforce obedience, or take action. It is the right to settle disputes, to control, and to make and implement decisions.

"People with authority include the President of the United States, the principal of a school, the head of a company, a parent, a coach, a policeman, a babysitter. Authority often gives people the right to make decisions for others, to manage a group, or to solve problems or disputes.

Power

"Some people who have little or no authority, still seem to have the power to lead others. **Power** may be defined as the ability or capacity to act in ways that influence the behavior of others. It is a personal talent that can be developed. Personal power is your ability to influence others. Power is earned through developing the trust, admiration and respect of others. It is entirely possible to possess a great deal of power, while not possessing any authority. Some people refer to this as charisma, a rare quality or power attributed to those persons who have demonstrated an exceptional ability for winning the devotion of large numbers of people. It is also possible to have the authority, but not the power.

"People of equal position and authority do not necessarily possess the same degree of power. The difference does not depend on the position or rank, but rather upon the individual. The effectiveness of a leader can be equated to the amount of personal power he or she has acquired."

Confusing? Not really. Let's take a minute to think it through. I'll help to explain and clarify the importance of each role. It will give you a clearer picture of how certain people really can be in charge and some just can't seem to 'get it.'

"Authority is very necessary and important. It helps maintain order in organizations and society. It can be efficient and powerful in maintaining order and achieving goals. A leader should not avoid the use of authority when the situation demands it, but should avoid creating situations in which authority is the only option.

"An individual who abuses authority diminishes his or her personal power, and ultimately, the ability to influence and lead others. A leader who possesses power only uses authority as a last resort to achieve goals. If you have earned the power by creating a climate of trust, permitting and helping others to maintain their dignity, their pride, and their autonomy, people will work and achieve because of the value they place on themselves. When you have earned this power, you must always be aware of the importance of your influence and always use it in a positive ways. The minute you misuse your power, there will be consequences, and it will take a long time for people to trust you again. I am convinced that leadership is found in the person, not in the position.

"Some people that come to mind as examples of the influences of power and authority are Mahatma Gandhi, Martin Luther King, Jr., Mother Theresa of Calcutta, and Nelson Mandela. These leaders earned the respect and admiration of millions of people and did not abuse any authority they might have had. They had acquired the necessary power to make sweeping changes in the world. Do you wonder how they did it? They found the leader within themselves and found the courage to act on it. They didn't just think about it, but they took action. And that's what made the difference."

Now, for a "regular" kind of guy...

My friend and fellow Rotarian, Joe Kelly, is an amazing person. He has an unbelievable passion for young people. He comes about this "honestly." Joe will now share with us a turning point in his young life, why he is the way he is and what it means to him and others he comes in contact with:

Joe Kelly

"When I was teenager, one of my teachers nominated me for a Student of the Month Award. I was a straight-A student and was involved in sports and community activities. I kind of thought that this was a long shot; after all, I attended Dudley High School, and there were not too many of the students who went there that got much recognition, no matter what they accomplished. So you can imagine how surprised I was when I found out that I had actually won! This was life changing for me. Someone really cared; someone had taken notice of my efforts. It didn't matter what school I attended. I was encouraged to continue on this positive path... after all, someone *had* noticed and maybe others were noticing, too. Besides, it was really nice to have Dudley High School in the spotlight for a change. I'll never forget the impact this had on my life.

"This award was given by a Rotary Club in my city. To think that an organization made up of successful business men really did care about the youth of the city had me curious, and I researched this organization. What kinds of other programs did they offer to encourage youth to be successful? I planned to take advantage of all they offered. And I did.

"Today I am a proud Rotary member and have been for 11 years. From the very beginning, I got involved in any activity or program that was related to youth. I was determined to make a difference in the lives of as many kids that I could. I have risen up in the ranks, and I was privileged to have been elected to more and more influential positions within the hierarchy of the Rotary organization. As a Rotarian, I use my positions to do whatever I can so that youth in challenging socio-economic situations can aspire to a better quality of life. I am proud to be an advocate for youth. I have chaired committees such as the Student Improvement Awards Committee, and I have helped improve living conditions of homes that some of these kids live in, through our Project Rebuild program. Interacting and reading with students as part of one of the reading programs at one of our elementary schools, is a way that I can do my part for the students, thereby increasing their chances for a more successful school year. Today, the Student Improvement Award goes to students who are not necessarily getting the highest grades or are best at their sports, but to those who have truly shown steady improvements in their lives.

"I enjoy partnering with Youth First, an organization in our city that is part of the Parks and Recreation division, which was awarded a grant, making it possible to form a Youth Basketball League and Football League. Through these leagues, more than 600 boys and girls from 4 –16 years old, learn and participate in a sport they thought they might never have the opportunity to play. I also enjoy coaching these young people. Getting the grant was great, but nothing beats being right there in the thick of things with these kids. I want them to know that they are important and someone other than, let's say family members, cares enough to coach them and simply be there for them. They need someone to cheer for them and also to be there when they do not win.

"As president of Summit Rotary in 2006–2007, I used my position to encourage the members to be very involved in many activities, especially the youth activities. I still enjoy leadership positions in Rotary International. I am now an Assistant to the District Governor. I want to continue to make a difference in the lives of as many children and families as I can. I am told that I have influence because my passion and enthusiasm are contagious and people want to help me and enjoy being part of my teams as we help in endeavors to make a difference in people's lives. I consciously make the Rotary's Four Way Test a part of my daily life: "Of all things we think, say or do—Is it the TRUTH? Is it FAIR to all concerned? Will it build GOODWILL and BETTER FRIENDSHIPS? Will it be BENEFICIAL to all concerned?" The Rotary's Four Way Test guides me to be a good, strong leader.

"It also keeps me focused on "Service Above Self." One should never attempt to serve others while secretly desiring recognition from anybody. That defeats the purpose of our Motto and our Four Way Test. We feel and share the power that service performed with sincerity and humility brings. It is a true leader who knows that the betterment of those we serve is our true reward. That is true power."

Power is the reward for doing things right, and for doing the right things.

Thank you, Joe, for using your positions of authority and power to make big differences in people's lives. You truly deserve a round of applause! Take an extra bow!

If you are interested in learning more about Rotary International, please visit: www.rotary.org

Leadership Qualities

Believe it or not, someone is always watching you and learning from you. It is important to work at being your best to be the person you aspire to be.

Develop your personal power. Celebrate your accomplishments. Focus on your strengths. Inspire those around you. Believe in yourself and others will believe in you, too.

So... You need to choose to develop the qualities that will make you an influential leader and make them an integral part of your life.

Some of these **qualities** are:

Self-esteem: Unless you love yourself, it will be very difficult to love others. Appreciate your value as a human being.

Empathy and Understanding: Empathy is the ability to put yourself in someone else's shoes, to understand. It means neither agreement nor disagreement, rather understanding why people feel the way they do.

Self-confidence: Have faith in yourself. Build on your successes and learn from your setbacks. Know that you have the potential to succeed.

Courage: Facing the unknown, risking failure, and stepping out of your comfort zone are all actions that require courage. Have the courage to also do what is right.

Self-discipline: Practice what you preach. Walk the talk.

Positive mental attitude: This is a foundation for successful leadership and for all sustained achievement. Consciously seek out people and circumstances that will reinforce your positive attitudes.

Integrity: This may well be the most important quality you can develop as a leader, and as an individual. It is the quality that gives meaning to all the rest of your achievements. It is associated with honesty, accountability, high standards, and clearly defined values. Developing these qualities will increase your personal power and give you much deserved self-pride.

Let me introduce you to another friend and colleague of mine, Debra Vigliano, Founder and Executive Director of Win-Win Resolutions, Inc. She does amazing things with youth, helping them develop skills that will allow them to be leaders, possibly even in positions of authority and or power. She also has added a family program and a corporate program to further instill these all-important ideals. Many times the adults need to be empowered to be leaders so they can more effectively empower their children. Debra is a person that the youth and adults look to as an authority figure, but she also has earned the power to be effective with the people she serves. Debra, please share more with us about you and your amazing program:

Debra Vigliano

"Theater is one of my passions. Youth is another. I wanted to combine both of these passions so that young people could benefit from my talents. The concept was developed as part of my graduate school studies and then was successfully implemented as a pilot program in the Guilford County School System in 1998. The rest, as they say, is history. Since Win-Win Resolutions started in 2001, over 30,000 students (Pre-K to twelfth grade) have benefited from our conflict resolution training.

"I have over thirty years experience as a theater educator and program director. Interactive drama is a wonderful way to teach skills to youth so they can become empowered to make the necessary changes in their lives and help others do the same. The experiences of acting out the situations, trying them on for size, as they become more comfortable with saying and using these success skills, allows them to internalize the processes so that they becomes an integral part of their everyday lives. Our primary mission in our organization is to reduce violence and prejudice in schools and communities by teaching conflict resolution and positive social skills through interactive drama. Our staff of theatre teachers and professional counselors guides students to develop positive interactive skills that they will continue to use throughout their lives, specifically focusing on the areas of anger management, preventing rumors that escalate into violence, and reinforcing the importance of respecting each other by embracing our diversity. We tend to focus on crucial areas of student development, such as: creative problem-solving, self-awareness, team work, self-esteem, and communication tools.

"Win-Win Resolutions started out focusing solely on students. We have now expanded to include Family and Corporate Conflict Resolution Training so all family members are given the opportunity to have a shared experience and develop a common vocabulary. The myriad of pressures at work, at home, and in society have made this a welcome addition to the adult world. The more we know about ourselves and issues that trigger anger and emotional responses and learn how to effectively react in a proactive, civilized, and respectful manner, the better off our community and greater society will be. I'm just thankful that I can offer these additional programs."

Thank you, Debra, for all the valuable services you are providing for our community and helping people become empowered for success. You absolutely deserve a round of applause! If you are interested in learning more about this program, please visit www.winwinresolutions.org.

I challenge you to rise up to the occasion. You are worth it! You will hear applause!

Who in your life has made a difference or had an impact on your life? How?

_____

_____

_____

Can you think of other people that have effectively mastered the art of authority and power? How have they done this?

_____

_____

_____

What are some of your values that you are especially proud of which you have developed and incorporated into your daily life?

_____

_____

_____

What areas do you find yourself needing more work or development? What are you planning on doing about it?

_____

_____

_____

"I'm Okay" by Styx

Submitted by Jan McDiarmid, Greensboro, North Carolina

"Be yourself, whatever that might be. Be true to yourself.
Don't try to live up to others' expectations."

Jan is the owner of Digital Introductions – developing
and producing video business cards, web video
presentations, personalized flashdrives, video e-mail,
video real estate tours, and video testimonials.

Learn more at: www.digitalintros.com and/or
digitalintroductions@gmail.com

"You Have To Believe You Are Magic" by Olivia Newton John

Submitted by Linda Brooks, Greensboro, North Carolina

"I chose this song because it always come to mind
when things are not going as well as I would like.
It reminds me to be thankful for my talents and my
blessings. It gives me hope and confidence."

Linda is a certified reboundologist, a NEEDAK Soft-
Bounce Rebounder dealer, and a nutrition educator.

Learn more at: www.2rebound.com
and/or reboundvy@aol.com

Uniquely You

It always amazes me that with all the thousands upon thousands of people, animals, plants, rocks, and minerals on this Earth—THEY ARE ALL UNIQUE!!!

Even identical twins are not identical. Snowflakes and raindrops, are not identical. We are all from an inspiration; we **are** an inspiration.

Success Mantra

Because you are unique, I hope you will keep this in mind as you choose to say this mantra:

I CHOOSE TO:

SEIZE THE DAY!
because

I EXPECT SUCCESS!
because

I AM WORTH IT!
because

I HAVE PERSONAL POWER!
because

I WANT TO HEAR APPLAUSE!

For this chapter, I am choosing to share this piece of writing from Virginia Satir, a noted American author and psychotherapist.

Hopefully you will also feel like I do, that the topics shared in this book are interwoven and expressed beautifully in her poem. I hope it inspires you to a deep appreciation of your uniqueness. I hope it inspires you to greatness.

MY DECLARATION OF SELF-ESTEEM

I am me.

In all the world, there is no one else exactly like me.

There are persons who have some parts like me, but no one adds up exactly like me. Therefore, everything that comes out of me is authentically mine because I alone chose it.

I own everything about me—

my body, including everything it does;

my mind, including all its thoughts and ideas;

my eyes, including the images of all they behold;

my feelings, whatever they may be – anger, joy, frustration, love, disappointment, excitement;

my mouth, and all the words that come out of it, polite, sweet or rough, correct or incorrect;

my voice, loud or soft; and all my actions, whether they be to others or to myself.

I own my fantasies, my dreams, my hopes, my fears.

I own all my triumphs and success, all my failures and mistakes.

Because I own all of me, I can become
intimately acquainted with me.

By doing so, I can love me and be friendly
with me in all my parts.

I can then make it possible for all of me
to work in my best interests.

I know there are aspects about myself that puzzle
me, and other aspects that I do not know.

But as long as I am friendly and loving to myself, I can
courageously and hopefully look for the solutions to the
puzzles and for ways to find out more about me.

However I look and sound, whatever I say and do, and
whatever I think and feel at any given moment in time is me.

This is authentic and represents where
I am at that moment in time.

When I review later how I looked and sounded,
what I said and did, and how I thought and felt,
some parts may turn out to be unfitting.

I can discard that which is unfitting, and keep that which proved
fitting, and invent something new for that which I discarded.

I can see, hear, feel, think, say, and do.

I have the tools to survive, to be close to others, to
be productive, and to make sense and order out of
the world of people and things outside of me.

I own me, and therefore I can engineer me.

I am me, and I am okay.

"Yiheyeh Tov" by David Broza

Submitted by Gaby Mahalin, Jersey City, New Jersey

"There will always be challenges for us to face – disagreements, dangers, fights, wars, and other things in our lives that can add stress. However, this song is a song about peace and optimism and love and confidence that good will prevail."

Gaby is the general manager of White Gloves Moving and Storage.

Learn more at: www.whiteglovemoving.us and/or gaby@whiteglovemoving.us

"California Stars" by Billy Bragg and Wilco

Submitted by Monique La Perriere, Fort Collins, Colorado

"I chose this song because it helps me to slow down and consider the things in life that are important to me. It rouses memories of carefree days with friends and family and inspires me to balance my time and energy to make the best of love, adventure, career, and quiet. And…you can also substitute your own state's name and enjoy the song even more!"

Monique is an ecologist and lover of the outdoors. She is a writer-editor for the U.S. Forest Service in Fort Collins, Colorado and managing editor for Fire Management Today.

Stress!!! What's Stress Got to Do With It... Got To Do With It...

Stress. We're in denial of it because it represents loss of control. We use it as an excuse because it is something most people can relate to. We use it as a crutch to wrap our minds around life and hope to just get to the next step. However we look at it, and *stress* about it, stress is inevitably a part of our everyday life. Not dealing with it or denying it does not make stress go away. Stress can make us get old faster and stop us dead in our tracks or keep us young by using our brains and ingenuity to get beyond our stress factors.

Which choice is more appealing to you?

By the time you've reached this part of the book, I hope you have come to recognize the choices you have that can make your life more stress free and to recognize that YOU are worth the effort.

Habits & Hidden Potential, Ego-In a Positive Sense, Action Words, Reframe It!, Attitude, Perception, Positive Self-Talk, Laughter, Authority and Power, Uniquely You: these are ideas that have already been shared with you as choices to incorporate into your life. These new choices will help you deal with all the *buttons* that people can press to make your life miserable.

Linda Hamilton again reminds us that you cannot control all the stressors that could play havoc with your life; however, you can control how you react to these stressors. You can choose to react in a negative way such as drinking a bottle of wine…or 2… or 3… or going on a spending spree. Or you can choose to react in a positive way, maybe venting your frustrations by scrubbing the kitchen floor or cleaning your house or working in the garden. If you've chosen the negative approach, you'll probably wake up with a huge hangover or broke. If you've chosen the positive approach, you'll at least have a clean house or a pretty garden!

Possibly stress *is* already a little more under control; however, let's take some time to look at the basics that will give you more choices as you deal with stress.

What are some positive ways you can choose when dealing with stress? Practicing yoga, playing your favorite sport, exercising, cleaning, using breathing techniques, listening to calming music, singing your favorite songs at the top of your lungs, dancing up a storm, gardening, going for a long walk or bicycle ride, talking your problems out with a therapist or a coach, are just some suggestions that can work for you.

Unattractive negative ways that people might opt to use in dealing with stress could be reverting to drinking, using drugs, gambling, overspending, cursing or yelling at people, being unable to get out of bed, having panic attacks, abusing family members or animals, abusing prescription drugs, promiscuous sex, or not caring about how they look.

Young, Successful Executive Story

I'd like to share a story with you from an anonymous author about what can happen if you are stressed or always in a hurry:

A young and successful executive was traveling down a neighborhood street, stressed and going too fast in his new Jaguar. He was watching for kids darting out from between parked cars and slowed down when he thought he saw something. As his car passed, and no children appeared, a brick smashed into the Jag's side of the driver's door! The driver slammed on the brakes and backed the Jag back to the spot where the brick had been thrown.

The angry executive then jumped out of the car, grabbed the nearest kid and pushed him up against a parked car shouting, "What was that all about and who are you? Just what the heck are you doing? That's a new car and that brick you threw is going to cost me a lot of money. Why did you do that?"

The young boy was apologetic.

"Please, mister...I'm sorry but I didn't know what else to do," he pleaded. "I threw the brick because no one else would stop..."

With tears dripping down his face and off his chin, the youth pointed to a spot just behind a parked car. "It's my brother," he said. "He rolled off the curb and fell out of his wheelchair and I can't lift him up."

Now sobbing, the boy asked the stunned executive, "Would you please help me get him back in his wheelchair? He's hurt and he's too heavy for me."

Moved beyond words, the driver tried to swallow the rapidly swelling lump in his throat. He hurriedly but carefully lifted the handicapped boy back into the wheelchair, then took out his handkerchief and dabbed at the fresh scrapes and cuts. A quick look told him everything was going to be OK.

"Thank you and may God bless you," the grateful child told the stranger.

Too shook up for words, the man simply watched the boy push his wheelchair-bound brother down the sidewalk toward their home. It was a long, slow walk back to the Jag. The damage was very noticeable, but the driver never bothered to repair the dent in the door. He kept the dent there to remind him of this message:

Don't go through life so fast that someone has to throw a brick at you to get your attention!

Yes, it is OK to take the time necessary to slow down—stop even, assess the situation; proceed with caution at first, then do what has to be done with intention and right action.

A friend and colleague, Cathy Daniels-Lee, has made it one of her missions to help people learn and take the necessary steps to be successful, even thought life will sometimes throw a brick or two your way. Her experiences and expertise help to take some of the stress out of their daily lives. When you have the proper steps in place, there will be less stress. Cathy is involved with entrepreneurs on a professional level as well as with youth the high school level. Cathy will now share with us some of the reasons why she chose to do the things she does:

Cathy Daniels-Lee

"A good friend of mine recently told me that helping people start and grow businesses was my *ministry*. I had never thought about it that way, and was initially surprised by her statement. However, as her words replayed in my mind, I decided there was a great deal of truth in her observation. For the past two years I have had the title of Program Coordinator at the Nussbaum Center for Entrepreneurship in Greensboro, North Carolina. My responsibilities include coordinating workshops and directing small business owners to various resources to help grow their businesses. The Nussbaum Center is the largest business incubator in North Carolina, and we provide office space, mentoring, and workshops for entrepreneurs.

"I really find it interesting that I have a job which allows me to help people start and grow businesses. Although I owned a business many years ago, it did not do well. To be quite honest, over the years I have experienced far more failure in my life than success. I have a failed marriage and numerous failed relationships, both personal and professional. In addition, I have failed at jobs and regularly struggle in my role as a mother, daughter, and church member. So, why would a person with such a long history of failures and minimal entrepreneurial experience be charged with the responsibility of helping entrepreneurs achieve success? I ask myself that question often. However, as I look back over the past two years, I can in some ways see how I was called to serve small business owners and how all of my failures might actually be an asset.

"To the best of my knowledge, I'm the first person to have the responsibilities of a program coordinator at the center. I was originally hired to work at the front desk, but hated that position. Yet there was something exciting about being in the presence of so many people who worked diligently to turn their dreams of being entrepreneurs into a reality. There was a synergy I found inspiring. So instead of just sitting around hating my job, I decided to take on new responsibilities to make my days more interesting and rewarding. I attended numerous workshops provided by other organizations to expand my knowledge of the skills needed to start and grow a successful business. I also found that I really enjoyed sharing what I learned with aspiring entrepreneurs.

"In addition, I enjoyed talking to small business owners and learning the types of workshops they wanted. I also enjoyed developing relationships with the various people I asked to provide the workshops. The workshop facilitators, many of whom were business owners, were usually very generous with their knowledge.

"During my first year at the Nussbaum Center, it became apparent to me there were various segments of the population that were underserved. I guess the first step I took to address that issue was to collaborate with a couple of organizations and host a conference for women entrepreneurs in 2008. The majority of participants were African American women with lifestyle businesses that earned less than $10,000 annually. I was surprised and very pleased by the number of women who came out for this conference. They seemed so grateful for an opportunity to attend a number of different workshops and network with like-minded women. There was a synergy and excitement at the event that made all the hard work far more rewarding than I had anticipated. I was also very pleased that separate workshops for high school girls were included at the conference, and over forty students participated. Shortly after the conference, the Nussbaum Center collaborated with a local university to launch a networking group for women business owners entitled, Women's Entrepreneurial Leadership and Learning, WELL. The purpose of WELL was to provide workshops and networking opportunities for nascent and established women entrepreneurs. The workshops covered a variety of topics including marketing, branding, accounting practices, and online social networking.

"WELL provided a unique, up close and personal look at the challenges and triumphs many women business owners experience. It also enabled me to help many of the ladies on a variety of levels. Some needed help researching their market and benefited from learning information about Google's Wonder Wheel, Reference USA, and www.pew.org.

"Others wanted to obtain government contracts and I connected them with representatives at the Small Business Technology and Development Center, Small Business Transportation Resource Center, NC Military Business Center, etc. Still others had misconceptions about grants being available to for-profit businesses, and I regularly had to deliver the bad news that there are actually very few grants available to for-profit businesses.

"However, as I started to cultivate relationships with members of WELL, it became very apparent to me that helping entrepreneurs involved far more than just focusing on their business related needs and questions. There were times when I received calls or visits from women business owners in tears because a husband walked out and their business was not generating enough money to cover household expenses. Women confided in me when they were heartbroken, contemplating divorce or disillusioned by a failed relationship. There were women who asked for prayer because they received a dreaded diagnosis of cancer or that a parent was seriously ill. I got to hear the fear and sense of urgency in women's voices as the recession caused them to lose lucrative contracts and struggle with having to lay off employees or start looking for a job. More frequently, I received calls from ladies devastated after losing a well-paying job and desperate to start a business quickly in the hopes of replacing lost income.

"It was during the times women shared their personal setbacks, challenges, and heartaches that I was often able to provide compassion, support, and empathy. I was able to draw from the various challenges I had made it through to know how to listen and encourage others. I understand the emotional turmoil one goes through before accepting the fact a marriage is over and the frightening realities of starting a new life alone. I have been there. I know what it's like to lose a job and remain unemployed for months. Waking up each day with nothing to but look for a job can become overwhelming and frequently leads to depression. I have been there. I also know what it's like to invest more money than you really have into a business that doesn't succeed and the negative impact it can have on your family and finances. I have been there, too.

"So, it was during the times when I tried to support others through the valleys of life I realized all of my *not so great* experiences have given me a greater sensitivity when others are hurting or fall short. My failures actually increased my ability to listen, empathize, and encourage others. Equally as important, encouraging others through difficult situations helps me to feel encouraged and makes me even more grateful for all God has brought me through. As I tell others to be encouraged, it also encourages me. Many of the ladies I meet teach me such valuable lessons as I watch them endure the storms of life. I learn so much from their ability to persevere, remain optimistic, and pursue their dreams of becoming successful business owners regardless of the setbacks.

Over the last two years I have learned that with each failure comes valuable wisdom that often provides knowledge, hope, and encouragement to others. I have learned that it is possible to turn your failures into assets and help someone else achieve success."

Learn more about WELL at www.wellwoman.ning.com.

Now do you see why I asked Cathy to be part of my book, especially adding her experiences to the chapter on Stress? I am humbled by all she has accomplished and how she has helped others feel a sense of accomplishment. I am so honored to call her a colleague and friend. Cathy, may people continue to benefit and ease their stress through opportunities that you provide for them.

A Simple "NO"

The power of a simple **NO** can do wonders in relieving stress. I'm sure you've heard that it *is* possible to say no to people, and things really will be OK and life will continue because of it. You're probably thinking, "Yeah, really!"

You may even gain new respect as people realize that you value yourself enough to know what you can realistically do and realistically not do. Freedom to enjoy your life, your family and friends without feeling guilty is an added bonus. All it takes is a little practice. Say it with me...

"Thanks for asking me to help out at the fundraiser, Sue. **NO**, I can't realistically bake three dozen brownies for the bake sale this time. However, please keep me in mind for future events." (If your budget allows it, maybe offering a monetary donation to the cause would be an acceptable alternative.)

"**NO**, Tom, I realistically cannot drive you and your friends to the ballgame tomorrow night. Let's put our heads together and see how we can make this happen if it is that important to you that you go."

"Sounds like that party will be lots of fun, Jane. **NO**, I really need to pass this Biology test tomorrow so I'm choosing to study tonight."

Have you noticed the words *realistically* and *choosing* appearing in the responses? These are power words that deftly share with others that you are aware of responsibilities already on your calendar. It also shows respect for yourself and the person you are speaking with.

"No." **is** a complete sentence in and of itself. No explanations needed. Saying no is a useful skill to learn, takes practice, and you can do it pleasantly. No is really effective by itself, especially if the tone and the body language match the no just right. Besides, you will never please everyone, and accepting this will reduce the pressure you put on yourself.

Remember that you do not have to go into a litany of reasons why—*just say no!* I agree that it may feel difficult at first. No really is enough; otherwise, you get caught in the trap of volunteering or giving in, anyway.

What are some other scenarios you need to practice saying no to before they might arise? If you've heard it through other sources, be prepared to say no if you have to, *before* the request comes to you. Practice, practice, practice—until you are really comfortable with saying no.

Good for you! You are worth it! Is that a quiet internal applause I'm hearing?

Let's now take a different view of how saying no can have an impact on your professional life. You'll see how this will also spill over into your personal life. A friend and colleague of mine that

I've always admired for her humility, sense of humor and ready smile, business acumen, and community involvement, Adrienne Cregar Jandler came to the forefront in the news a couple of years ago when she and her company, Atlantic WebWorks, were selected for the 2008 American Business Ethics Award from the Foundation for Financial Service Professionals in the Small Business category. This is not some rinky-dink award. This is big-time stuff. The other two winners were General Mills, one of the world's leading food companies, and Daisy Brand, a midsize business that produces dairy products.

You're probably wondering what this has to do with relieving stress. Well, would you agree that when you have the courage to say no and choose to do the right thing because it is right, you have probably lessened the stress in your life? Adrienne was nominated by a client. She was picked because of her policies, including turning down work from her clients' competitors and following billing practices designed to benefit clients, even if it meant losing revenue. Yep, this sounds like the Adrienne I know! Adrienne, give us your take on all of this:

Adrienne Creger Jandler

"I attribute much of my commitment to ethical business practices to my upbringing. My parents have always encouraged me to do my best in all things and to treat people fairly and with respect. One of the strongest points my parents instilled in me is that happiness cannot be bought at any price. Riches can be lost as quickly as they're made, but someone's good name, or bad name for that matter, stays with him or her for a lifetime. These were some of the habits that are ingrained in me and are so much a part of who I am and what I do. These habits affect not only me, but everyone I come in contact with. These habits bring out the 'hidden potentials' not only in me, but in my company, my clients and the community.

"You can't lose sight in the tough times of who you are and what you stand for. It's easy to be ethical in the good times. It's the tough times that really require you to make the hard decisions. When life isn't so rosy, you have to look inside yourself and you have to think about how you and your company are going to respond to challenging situations. I don't regret taking a strong ethical stand with my business. Ethical choices are never convenient, when you think about it. It's not easy to say no to unethical business practices. Our core values are based on the golden rule and doing business the right way, not the easy way. We are firmly committed to doing what's right for our clients, staff, and community, even when we sacrifice short-term financial gains to do so. Our ethical business standards are incorporated into all aspects of Atlantic WebWorks today. Those standards are: Act in the best interest of the client at all times; invest in training and continuing education so clients receive the best possible services; offer courteous, timely support, and help clients understand how to use available technologies. We've found that making these choices has been the foundation for building trust. Our staff doesn't simply 'do the right thing' because it's expected. They do the right thing because they're personally committed to doing so. It keeps our clients coming back and this has helped us build a successful business over the long haul. It's our company policy, for example, not to build Web sites for the direct competitors of our clients, nor will we build Web sites that are pornographic in nature or are for organizations that promote discrimination, hatred, or harmful intent to any group of people or animal. We respect and value our partnerships with our clients. The ethical choices that I've chosen to make are, in my opinion, my small way of making the world the way I think it should be.

"Saying no to unethical practices is actually much easier than you may realize. It *is* an incredible stress-reliever...to know that you can look in the mirror and have no regrets. In addition, the people you respect—clients, friends, family, business partners—

have a greater trust in you when they know they can count on you to make the right decisions."

Thank you, Adrienne. What an inspiration…and for taking NO to a higher level. This is so refreshing to hear about, considering all the corporate scandals of greed and ego-boosting we are hearing so much about today. Even though times and jobs may change, business, as well as personal ethics, should never go out of style. OK, readers, I'm sure you have it in you to step up and do the same!

Adrienne, most definitely deserve a round of applause… maybe even a standing ovation.

Would you agree that Adrienne could have been part of the Habits & Hidden Potential Chapter as well as the Authority & Power Chapter? It is quite interesting how so many of these chapters are intertwined, that doing the right things all build on one another, and will eventually have you hearing applause.

Years ago someone shared this cute little letter with me. Do you think this father was comfortable with saying no? Read on:

Dear Dad,

$chool is really $well. I am making lot$ of friend$ and $tudying very hard. I have $o much $tuff, I $imply can't think of anything I need. $o if you like, $end me a card, a$ I would love to hear from you.

Love,

Your $on, $teve

Dear son,

I kNOw astroNOmy, ecoNOmics, and oceaNOgraphy are eNOugh to keep an hoNOrs student busy. Do NOt forget that the pursuit of kNOwledge is a NOble task, and you can't study eNOugh.

Love, Dad

(Oh my…Maybe this letter could have been part of the laughter chapter!)

I mentioned at the beginning of this book that I would be challenging you to think about ordinary things in extraordinary ways, ways that are not the usual way we tend to think of things or use them. A homophone is two or more words that are pronounced the same but differ in meaning, origin, and often spelling. Well, a homophone for **no** is **know**. So why am I going there? Well, would you agree that it would be easier to say *no* to something or someone if you *know* more about the subject, event, story, or person? No and know are powerful words. To *know* will give you courage, confidence, or an edge. To *know* is to learn, to teach, to share, to help, to excel, to be open-minded, to forge new paths. To *know* gives us the freedom to challenge ourselves. The *know* will make us feel more comfortable with uncomfortable situations that might require a *no*…or a yes. The more you know, the less stress there could be in your everyday life. So make sure you're "in the know" to make "saying no" a little easier.

Many of us think that an answer to someone's question or request must be given immediately. Oftentimes we feel cornered or trapped when we really need to say NO to the request or question. Asking for some extra time to think about your answer can take some pressure off and you now have time to think about the answer that will work best for you. Being specific about when you will have an answer for them, will make you look professional and responsible.

Talking about money tends to be a daunting conversation topic. It often adds a certain amount of stress to anyone's life. There are so many levels to dealing with money or finances. My friend Syble Solomon is an international speaker on the psychology of money. She shares that when it comes to money, our habits and attitudes can either support or sabotage our life, relationship, career, or financial goals. Many of our habits and attitudes are related to money and tend to affect how, why, when, or where we spend, save, give, invest, or go into debt. She feels very strongly about the effects of money on our lives. So much so, that she has created and developed a game-like tool called *Money Habitude*s. Using this particular deck of cards is a fun, non-judgmental and constructive way to talk about money. This game can be used in a family setting, in a classroom, with couples, or in discussion groups as a stand-alone activity. Interested? Visit her website at: www.moneyhabitudes.com and see if this will help to make a positive difference in your life by relieving some of your financials stressors.

We've discussed the paradigm shift of time management to meaning self-management. Time is something we can't control; however, we *can* control how we use our time and how we use it determines our overall success in what we are endeavoring to do. You do not have to squeeze everything possible into a day. It is perfectly reasonable and acceptable to ink in some downtime during the day (that's right, not pencil in; it's too easy to erase pencil markings) so you can refresh yourself and recharge your batteries. Be purposeful with your time. Instead of booking every minute of your day, leave some time open when you can catch up on anything new that comes in or deal with old items that have been hanging around. Also, don't forget to leave time for traveling from one location to another, keeping in mind traffic and other emergencies that might arise. Another suggestion might be that at the end of each day, map out a plan for the next day or two. When you can see clearly what is happening over the next two or three days ahead of you, you'll find that you are much less vulnerable to feeling overwhelmed, and you'll be better able to deal with challenges that arise. You cannot change time, yet you can make changes to your time by organizing yourself, setting priorities, and taking responsibility. Think of how much more effective you could be! When you manage yourself you will have more time to create the life you really want. You will accomplish far more on a daily basis. Research is proving more and more how multi-tasking and cramming too much into a day actually makes you much less effective. Do you ever feel like your short-circuiting? There are times I feel like I do! Yet, when you are more in control of your time, you will find that there might even be a change in your body language, tone of voice, and your demeanor. You may be smiling more. You may wonder where your headaches went. You may be enjoying your family or work more.

"Keeping up with the Joneses" is not all that it's cracked up to be! Respect yourself and your time and others will value you also. Making yourself a priority on your to-do list does not lessen the importance of other people or happenings in your life. It just puts things in the right perspective.

Sherré DeMao is an author, speaker, entrepreneurial business expert, as well as a colleague and friend of mine. In her book, *Me, Myself & Inc.*, she challenge us with these affirmations or self-promises: Promise #1: I will either find a way or make a way; Promise #2: I will not feel guilty about making life easier for myself; and Promise #3: I will keep my mind open to all possible support and resources. As you give yourself permission to put these promises into action, you will discover that you are in a better place to be at your best at all times.

Believe it or not, you *can* ask for help. Remember the *Ego* Chapter? Many times we put ourselves in impossible situations because of our ego and how we want to be perceived.

Time Management

Let's do some *paradigm shifting.* I will paraphrase an article written by Barbara Hustedt Crook that I read in the February 1, 2010 issue of *Woman's World* magazine.

You think: "I don't want to impose." Actually: People really want to help. People enjoy feeling needed. Most people are flattered to think that they are talented enough for the task. This also shows that you are confident enough in yourself and or your relationship to ask for their help.

You think: "I'll look weak or needy." Or "I'll look incompetent or lazy." Actually: Asking for help is a sign of strength and empowerment. The fact that you have this self-awareness to know that a situation or problem can be better taken care of or solved by someone capable of helping you, lets people believe that you deserve help. This can also be interpreted as delegating and being a part of a team. You'll be seen as professional and efficient. It makes you seem more human and likable and shows that you have good time-management skills. You just need their expertise to make it happen.

Speaking of delegating…Take the time to teach your children, your students, or the people you work with how to do things, and how to do them well. Make it your responsibility to demonstrate and set a standard that you will find acceptable and will meet your expectations. This takes you from a "Cinderella" state of mind to a "CEO" state of mind. Some positive outcomes of this type of thinking are: people learn how to do tasks more effectively, learn how to do new tasks, have more of a sense of ownership, develop more of a team spirit, develop more self-confidence, have less of a sense of entitlement...and you get to get more things done and have more time! What's not to like about this?

S.M.A.R.T. Goals

Another stress-relieving suggestion is goal setting. You're probably thinking this activity is going to *add* stress to your life — where are you going to find time for that, for goodness sake!?!

Really, goal setting is SMART, relieves stress and can help you manage your time — OOPS! I mean *yourself* - more wisely.

Stress is leaving things to chance. Instead of relying on fate, reduce your stress and take control. Determine your future and the accomplishments it will bring.

Setting goals helps you prioritize and gives you a clearer picture of what you value most. You may discover that certain goals are in conflict with each other. This is where your values system kicks in as a base for understanding and setting your goals. Goal setting prompts you to take action. It helps you overcome obstacle. It helps you visualize the end product and the benefits and rewards you will enjoy. It is meant to produce results. The more **your** goals are truly **your** goals, the more likely you will be successful in accomplishing them. You can listen to others and learn from them, but make decisions based upon what you know to be right for you.

So let's get **S.M.A.R.T!**

S: State your goals positively and specifically. When the goal is stated positively and specifically, you have increased your chances for success by quite a bit because your brain can now produce a mental picture of what you want to do. We've discussed this concept in previous chapters. A goal stated negatively short-circuits the brain and decreases the chance of successfully getting the desired results. You must be able to visualize what you want

TO DO. When you visualize the desired outcome, it's much easier to put a plan in place and act on it.

For instance, if your goal is to stop missing free throws, you need to see yourself shooting baskets. The goal statement might read: "I will practice as much as I need to in order to get baskets and score for my team when we play Central High." This will be more effective since you can now see and feel and visualize the goal.

M: Goals should be measurable. For example, what are the parameters you are setting for yourself? Is it a noticeable increase in your salary? Is it a noticeable positive growth in your relationship with someone? Is it increased productivity? Are your grades improving?

A and R: Are your goals attainable and realistic? It's good to challenge yourself and go out of your comfort zone, but your goals do need to be attainable and realistic if you work hard enough and stretch yourself a bit. If your goals are too high, you may find yourself procrastinating and not even achieving the lowest objective of your goal.

T: The power of a deadline...Goals should be *time bound*, have a beginning and an end. Have a beginning date and a projected finish date for each step of your action plan. Goals, whether they are short-term goals or long-term goals, should have a deadline. This adds a sense of urgency to your activity level and increases the chances for your achieving those goals. Also, visualizing the outcome and putting realistic time settings on what you want to accomplish ramp up your performance as you tackle the obstacles in your action plan.

I also like to add a **Y,** making it SMARTY goals. The goals need to be **yours.** You can have long lists of goals, but if they are not your goals and you do not have an emotional attachment to them, it will be more of a challenge to accomplish them. Why would you really want to do this? What would drive you to do that? Is it worth it to you as well as to someone else? After all, you will be investing time and effort accomplishing these goals.

Let's go back to the goal that was stated earlier in this section and turn it into a SMARTY goal:

"I will practice shooting baskets two hours each day after school so that I can help my team score when we play Central High next week."

Do you think this person will be more motivated and will ultimately hear applause?

Another result or reward of a SMARTY goal is that it encourages you to focus not only on yourself, but on others and the grand scheme of things.

Now you it's your turn to think of a goal you would like to see yourself achieving and write it down as a SMART goal. You can do it!

_____

_____

_____

My friend, Nathan Wainscott, had a dream that required some serious goal planning. His dream is to open a music center for youth so that they will have a safe place to develop their music abilities or simply have a place to go to enjoy music. He also sees this as a haven where positive conditions will help prevent drug and alcohol abuse. Nathan's long-range goal started with several short-range goals so he would have a system and a logical plan in place that would allow him to pursue this dream in a SMARTY way. Here he is, sharing his story with us:

"I started thinking about a music incubator about six years ago. It was a lofty dream—the 'YMCA' of music. I called it Musicians Anonymous and even sketched out a floor plan on trace paper.

Nathan Wainscott

But this idea simply collected dust on my desk, elbowed aside by my daily grind of duties as a father, husband, and owner of a decorative painting company. Then, one evening, after tucking the kids into bed, my wife, Melodie, and I were watching the local news, and I heard someone say something about a Mrs. Rizzo. That's when something clicked; that name 'Rizzo' brought back a flood of memories. 'Oh my God,' I said to my wife. 'That's it! The Marcus C. Rizzo Center for Musician Enrichment. That's what it's going to be, honey—that's it!' Needless to say, my wife thought I was a bit loopy and just needed some sleep.

"I stayed up until four in the morning, poring through my old plans, as I remembered Marc Rizzo, the front man of our old garage band, Bipolar Disorder. As a teenager, I idolized Rizzo. He was two years older; he was a true 'guitar hero' before the game ever came out, and he played snare drum in Western Guilford High's marching band. But there was also something else. Rizzo was just so cool in that rock'n roll sort of way.

"But less than a year after graduating, Rizzo fatally shot himself in his apartment. He was eighteen. No note. No explanation. No nothing.

"I now find myself, nearly sixteen years later, beginning to understand the root cause of that seemingly impossible dream that was planted deep inside of me. I would turn the heartache of Rizzo's tragic loss into a heartfelt passion that would drive me toward the goal of opening a music center for youth. I approached Rizzo's family with my idea. They gave me their blessing. I approached city leaders; they offered me their support. I approached people like retired UNCG professor Bob Gingher, a board member with the Music Academy of North Carolina; he jumped on board to help. Then I pulled out my old, hand-sketched floor plan and realized the very place I was renting to run my paint business was the exact floor plan I sketched out on this frayed paper a few years ago! Coincidence? I…don't… think…so.

"Amidst all my other responsibilities, today I am the program facilitator of a non-profit …YES! You guessed it! It's The Marcus C. Rizzo Center for Musician Enrichment. It targets youth with an interest in music but without the means to explore their talent in a structured musical environment. We don't know whether or not an individual child will become a great musician. We can provide that child with goals, with a future enhanced by the unique sensitivity afforded by music. Our structure is designed to be an all encompassing community enrichment and musical arts incubation center. While working to strengthen and unite the social activities of an expanding culturally diverse population, we shall provide a safe place for our youth and local community to explore, enjoy and give back their matchless gift of music. There is even a leadership component that will encourage positive behavior as the musicians strive towards their goals.

"I estimate that it will take about $500,000 to open its doors. It's a lofty dream, but someone has to dream it into fruition…and I KNOW I'm not alone; divine hands are at work here."

Today the Marcus C. Rizzo Center for Musician Enrichment is becoming a reality; check it out at: www.rizzocenter.com. The results will be far-reaching and life changing for many youth. Following a very specific goal plan is part of his plan for the success of this dream he has. Please join me in giving Nathan a well-deserved round of applause!

My friend and colleague, Sharon Eden, (www.sharoneden.biz) likes to remind me of one last stress relief—and that is simply "to remember that *everything is as it needs to be*. Enjoy the ride as you learn to ride the crest of unpredictability, of uncertainty, of the reality of *life* as it is. The truth is that you and I cannot know what's going to happen in the next minute, let alone in the days ahead…even if it seems we ought to, especially with all the technological advances of today."

So stop a while and take time to *smell the flowers*. Take a deep breath. Be thankful and applaud the Universe for all your blessings.

What do you think are your stressors on your life, personal as well as professional?

_____

_____

What elements in your personal as well as your professional life do you feel are in your control? Why? What have you done to make this so?

_____

_____

_____

What elements in your personal as well as in your professional life are out of your control? Why? How does that make you feel? Is this something that you think you can change?

_____

_____

_____

Is it hard for you to delegate? Why?

_____

_____

_____

Which projects will you be delegating so that others, as well as yourself, will experience feelings of success?

_____

_____

"Defying Gravity" from the musical Wicked

Submitted by Jenny Telwar, Nashville, Tennessee

"This song gets me going and makes me feel like I can accomplish anything. It is the theme song for my business! The words resonate with empowerment, change, trusting your instincts, and doing the impossible - by defying gravity to unlimited greatness. Here's to new heights!"

Jenny is the CEO/Owner of the America's National Teenager Scholarship Organization.

Learn more at: www.nationalteen.com and/or jennytelwar@me.com

"One Moment in Time" by Whitney Houston

Submitted by Barbara Toscano, Ramsey, New Jersey

"This song is often heard during the U.S. Olympics broadcasting, and although we do not all compete in the Olympics, we all have goals and dreams…we face challenges as we strive to achieve them…and need to recognize our accomplishments when we do. Believe in yourself, and rejoice at being the best you can be!"

Barbara works with organization and individuals, adults or teens, offering leadership development, consulting, and personal coaching. She is President of Evolution, Inc.

Learn more at: www.successfulevolution.com and/or barbara@successfulevolution.com

Expect Success!

Create excitement! Make people stand up and take notice!

Create an impression! Expect success!

Throughout this book, I have shared one of the most important rules of success: begin with the end in mind.

When you can envision and just about feel the results you are working toward, it becomes easier to write the goal plans down and implement the action plans that will make it all happen.

You *can* expect success because you are better prepared to deal with the obstacles are in your way. You have also come to realize that you do not have to do anything alone—that you can always find support from family, friends, coworkers, and maybe even a coach.

It becomes easier to do an internal search for your hidden potential, and to develop the habits that will give you the personal power your new self will enjoy. There is a hidden bonus to your becoming more successful—your success ripples out to others who then become encouraged to empower themselves and others.

For this book, I deliberately chose people that I knew in my community in order to show how often we forget to look close to home for inspiration, that it really is possible for regular people to have an incredible impact on themselves, as well as on others in their families, communities and also abroad. The folks I introduced you to in my book—Kristen, Jan, Bill, Lisa D., Linda, Susan, Kate, Sue, Joan, Cindie, LaToya, Lisa F., Witt, Angel, Erinn, Joe, Debra, Cathy, Adrienne, and Nathan—are ordinary people doing extraordinary things with their lives. They are tapping into their talents and strengths. They have **chosen** to do the extra things that enable them to be empowered, to reach their dreams and goals, and on the way, make a difference in the lives of so many people. They have discovered the true meaning of *ego*. You can probably come up with examples of your own of ordinary people that you know of that are doing extraordinary things. Don't hesitate to thank them and share how much you appreciate their inspiration. Learn from them and then become extraordinary in your own way.

We are known by the company we keep. The company we keep ought to inspire us and invigorate us to greatness. Let us experience success by association. The people who strive for personal excellence will find a way to rub shoulders with the great people around them.

This brings the book full circle. In the rock climbing section, I mentioned the importance of "roping up" in life with other inspiring, motivating people. I like to call the contributors to my book, *Leona's Leaders*, because they lead me, they challenge me, and they inspire me to be the best that I can be for me…and others.

As you apply the use of action words, affirmations, and reframing to your success repertoire, your perception of yourself will change. You will see that you are no slouch as you stand tall with self-confidence, self-esteem, and self-respect.

Knowing the difference between authority and power will give you an edge as you work yourself up the ladder of success. People will be impressed with how well you are now dealing with stress in your life and a new found respect will put a smile on your face. Laughter and joy are now more a part of your daily life as your new attitudes lead you to higher altitudes. You revel in all of your unique qualities.

And…Good for you…

You are Hearing Applause!

Please use this book often as a stepping stone that will inspire you to read more, explore more intimately, discover the many ways that you can take charge of your life and delve deeper into the wonderful mystery of you.

Thank you for allowing me to be a part of the exciting journey of YOU!

And…Don't forget to share your stories with me for a future book.

And now for the "icing on the cake"…

We have just started on a journey together. As you reflect upon the success steps we shared in this book, why not take some time to pour yourself a cup of coffee, or a cup of tea, or a glass of wine and let this music flow over you as you relax.

My friend, Kellen Nelson from Fort Collins, Colorado shared this with me:

"During my childhood and adolescence, I was exposed to a lot of classical music. Much of it went in one ear and out of the other but a few composers stuck with me as my favorites. One of them is Gabriele Faure. Faure is a French composer who wrote primarily during the Romantic Period and is well known for the emotion of his music. The *Violin Sonata No. 1 in A (Op. 13) for Violin and Piano* really reminds me of the triumphs and struggles that take place when working toward and accomplishing a goal. *Movement 1* embodies all the blind optimism and enthusiasm that accompanies the new goal.

"*Movement 2* resounds with insecurity and the accompanying difficulties that come with realizing what you've taken on and how much work will be required to achieve it. *Movements 3* and 4 return to a cheerful theme that builds unto a loud, confident achievement. Certainly *Movement 2* couldn't happen without the naivety in *Movement 1*, and *Movement 3* and *Movement 4* wouldn't seem so grand without the depression in *Movement 2*.

"Perhaps my interpretation of this music fits your perspective on highs and lows of pursuing and achieving goals. Just remember to never give up!"

Kellen is a climber, skier, and forest biologist.

"You need to be aware of what others are doing, applaud their efforts, acknowledge their successes, and encourage them in their pursuits. When we all help one another, everybody wins."

Jim Stovall

Resources

Crook, Barbara Hustedt. "Want More Help? Just Ask!" **Woman's World**. 1 February 2010: 22

DeMao, Sherré. **Me, Myself & Inc.** Denver, NC: GreenCastle Publishing, 2009 (pp. 17-20)

Diaz, Monica with Susan Mazza. "When Being Positive Can Cost You". 15 January 2010. http://www.e-quidam.com/theblog

Hampton, Linda. "How Do You React to Stress?" 7 July 2009. http://clicks.aweber.com/y/ct/?1=BIKL_7m=1pBIubm13fPURm&b=dwCf7jRLLLUHNM6HHBKetA

"Id, ego, and super-ego." Wikipedia. 18 April 2009. http://en.wikipedia.org/wiki/EGO

"Laughter is the Best Medicine." HELP GUIDE.ORG. 13 July 2009. http://www.helpguide.org/life/humor_laughter_health.htm

Loomans, Diane with Julia Loomans. **100 Ways to Build Self-Esteem and Teach Values.** New York: MJF Books, 1994

"Playful Communication in Relationships." HELPGUIDE.ORG. 13 July 2009. http://www.helpguide.org/mental/eq7_playful_communication.htm

Resource Associates Corporation Rising Stars Leadership Process Manual. (2007). Mohnton, PA: Resource Associates Corporation (pp. 47, 53, 71, 122, 123, 125,151, 154, 155)

Resource Associates Corporation Rising Stars Implementation Guide. (2000). Mohnton. PA: Achievement Seminars International, Inc.

Resource Associates Corporation Executive Leadership Development Manual. (2002). Mohnton, PA: Resource Associates Corporation

Second College Edition of The American Heritage Dictionary. (1985). Boston: Houghton Mifflin Company

Solovic, Susan Wilson. **The Girls' Guide to Power & Success.** New York: MJF Books, 2001

Stout, James Harvey. "The Ego." 18 April 2009. http://www.theorderoftime.com/politics/cemetery/stout/h/ego.htm

"Transactional Analysis." Businessballs.com. 15 December 2009. http://www.businessballs.com/transact.htp

Williamson, Marianne. **A Return to Love: The Reflections on the Principles of *A Course in Miracles*.** New York: Harper Perennial, 1992 (pp.190, 191)

Leona's Leaders

In order of appearance:

Kristen Barbee
Assistant Youth First Coordinator
Greensboro Parks and Recreation Department
Folk Teen Center, 3910 Clifton Road, Greensboro, NC 27407
Ph: (336) 373-7710 Fax: (336) 373-2128
kristen.barbee@greensboro-nc.gov

Jan Clifford
Executive Director of HORSE**POWER**
Horsepower, Inc. Therapeutic Learning Center
8001 Leabourne Road, Colfax, NC 27235
Ph: (336) 931-1424 Fax: (336) 931-1425
www.horsepower.org
jan@horsepower.com

Bill Mangum
William Mangum Fine Art
2166 Lawndale Drive, Greensboro, NC 27408
Gallery: (336) 379-9200 Fax: (336) 273-2425
www.williammangum.com
bill@williammangum.com

Lisa Dames
Country music singer
P.O. Box 10665, Greensboro, NC 27404
www.lisadames.com
lisa@lisadames.com

Linda Blumenfeld
Owner of LBL Marketing, Inc.—affordable
marketing solutions with a "big business" feel.
She is also the marketing and account executive
for the Men Today magazine.
P.O. Box 6721, Summerfield, NC 27358
Ph: (336) 549- 8921
opbylinda@aol.com

Susan Midgett
S.O.S. For Haiti
816 Bass Landing Place, Greensboro, NC 27455
Ph: (336) 288-8998
www.sosforhaiti.blogspot.com
somidgett@aol.com

Sue Falcone
"Simply" Sue—A Speaker Who Writes
Motivational & Inspirational Speaker, Teacher, &
Author
5609 Landerwood Drive, Greensboro, NC 27405
Ph: (336) 375-1218 Toll-free: (888)766-3155
www.simplysuespeaks.com
simplysue@att.net

Joan Calvert
Community Service Representative for Home
Instead Senior Care & Ultimate "Networther"
Ph: (336) 312-2721
www.homeinstead.com
jcalvert@homeinstead.com

Cindie Brown
Cindie has an interest in conservative political
causes, such as Right to Life.
scotbrown@thejohnsonfinancialgroup.com

LaToya Marsh
Reigning Miss Greensboro
Areas of Expertise: marketing, promotions, event
planning, non-profit, fashion/entertainment/
sports. Experience includes: acting, casting,
pageants, judging, modeling
Ph: (336) 508-5179
missgreensboro@yahoo.com

Lisa Freeman
"Creating Healthier Lives"—Shaklee
7721 Fording Bridge Road, Kernersville, NC 27284
Ph: (336) 306-3892
http://freeman-associates.myshaklee.com
lfreeman@triad.rr.com

Angel Guerrero III
Owner of As Web Pros.com—a full service internet marketing, web design, e-commerce, hosting Content Management systems & SEO specialist firm
Ph: (336) 508-5870
www.aswebpros.com
angel@aswebpros.com

Erinn Diaz.
First In Flight Entertainment—your premier source for customized entertainment in North Carolina, providing professional entertainment of every kind for every occasion
P.O. Box 11012, Winston-Salem, NC 27116
Ph: (336) 924-7028 Fax: (954) 206-9529
www.FirstInFlightEntertainment.com
fifentertainment@yahoo.com

Joe Kelly
Owner of Awards of Excellence—trophies, plaques, certificates, awards, acrylic engraving, bronze castings, buttons, desk name plates
1027 E. Lindsay Street, Greensboro, NC 27405
Ph: (336) 274-6671 Fax: (336) 379-9218
www.awardsofexcellence.com
Trophy789@aol.com

Debra Viglione
Executive Director of Win-Win Resolutions—a nonprofit organization dedicated to violence prevention by developing conflict resolution skills using theatre education & peer mediation
122 N. Elm Street, Suite 516, Greensboro, NC 27401
Ph: (336) 230-1232 Fax: (336) 230-1236
www.winwinresolutions.org
debra@winwinresolutions.org

Cathy Daniels-Lee
Program Coordinator for the Nussbaum Center for Entrepreneurship; she leads the organization's education & networking group, Women's Entrepreneurial Leadership and Learning (WELL)
2007 Yanceyville Road, Greensboro, NC 27405
Ph: (336)371 -5001 Fax: (336) 379-5020
www.nussbaumcfe.com
cdanielslee@nussbaumcfe.com

Adrienne Crager Jandler
President, Atlantic WebWorks & Consulting, Inc.—builds your business on the web; turnkey development services include strategic & lifecycle planning, concept &design, development, hosting services; also comprehensive marketing, search engine optimization, & website maintenance programs
331 S. Swing Road, Greensboro, NC 27409
Ph: (336) 235-4011, X-102 Fax: (336) 235-4012
www.atlanticwebworks.com
ac@atlanticwebworks.com

Nathan Wainscott
Director, Marcus C. Rizzo Center for Musician Enrichment—everything an aspiring musician needs all in one place
P.O. Box 2644, Greensboro, NC 27402
Ph: (336) 362-1548
www.rizzocenter.com
nathan@inspiredbycolor.com

Song Submissions

Here are the other songs that were submitted for this book. All the songs that were submitted were great and this made the selection process quite challenging. Enjoy!

ALABAMA:

"Motions" by Matthew West and
"Slow Fade" by Casting Crowns

Submitted by **Misty Browning**, Decatur, Alabama

"These songs are representative of where I am in my life and how I'm feeling about it."

Misty is a pediatric chiropractor and the senior doctor at the Millar Chiropractic & Nutrition Center. She loves treating pregnant women and children.

Learn more at: www.millarchiro.com

ARKANSAS:

"I'm Still Standing" by Elton John

Submitted by **Marcia Cook**, Sherwood, Arkansas

"This is my favorite 'get my head back right again' song. The music is so upbeat that you can't keep still or keep from singing along. Of course, he's singing it because his lover has left and he wants her to know that he's not going to let that knock him down. I like to apply that to all the other 'junk' or little failures that I tend to let get in my way when they seem to try to knock me down."

Marcia is a business coach and owner of Pinnacle Performance Solutions. She helps people bridge the gap between where they want to be and where they are now. She specializes in helping companies develop LOYAL customers—not just satisfied ones.

Learn more at: www.pinnacleperformancesolutions.net and/or marcia@pinnacleperformancesolutions.net

CALIFORNIA:

"Hit Me with Your Best Shot" by Pat Benatar

Submitted by **Stephanie Chandler**, Gold River, California

"This song always gets my energy going. Maybe it's part of the entrepreneurial nature that we get knocked down and have to keep getting up again. All I know is that when it comes on in my car, I crank it up really loud and sing along!"

Stephanie is an author of several business and marketing books and she is also a speaker.

Learn more at: www.stephaniechandler. com; www.BusinessInfoGuide.com; www.AuthorityPublishing.com

FLORIDA:

"Three Little Birds" by Bob Marley and

"Man in the Mirror" by Michael Jackson

Submitted by **Donnal Chung**, Fort Myers, Florida

"'Three Little Birds' is one of my favorite 'get up and go' songs. Yes, I am a big Bob Marley fan and yes, my country of national origin is Jamaica. The song itself doesn't contain a lengthy vocabulary or great verbiage, but the message that it does send is very powerful in so much as it is short and sweet. The inspiration that comes from knowing that we get a new day every day when the sun rises and we shouldn't worry about anything is a powerful message."

Another one of my favorites is Michael Jackson's 'Man in the Mirror'—of course you just have to listen to the lyrics and you'll be motivated by that message. It's very, very provocative and stimulating."

Donnal is a coach with DMAccess International.

Learn more at: www.DMAccessInternational. com and/or dchung@dmaccess.biz

"Have I Told You Lately That I Love You" by Rod Stewart

Submitted by **Lisa Huetteman**, Tampa, Florida

"I actually have a dual purpose for that song. For 14 years, this was Scott's and my song. We danced to it at our wedding. It described our relationship. Then, at a turning point in my life, when I realized I wasn't putting God first and I started forging a personal relationship with Jesus, I realized then that it was my love song for Christ, too. It is a divine love and that helps ease me in troubled and happy times."

Lisa is a coach and a partner in organizational transformation with Black Diamond Associates. She is also an author of the forthcoming book: *The Value of Values: 5 Keys to Achieving Organizational Success through Values-Based Leadership.*

Learn more at: www.the-black-diamond.com and/or lisa@the-black-diamond.com

"You Gotta Make Your Own Sunshine" by Neil Sedaka

Submitted by **Tracy Lunquist**, DeLand, Florida

"This is the best song I've heard about taking responsibility for your own attitude. Complaining gets you nowhere fast. Pick yourself up, smile, and go on. The message is on target and the mood of the song is so upbeat that I can't help but feel terrific anytime I hear it."

Tracy is the President of Working Magic, a business coaching and people development company.

Learn more at: www.workingmagic.net and/or tracy@workingmagic.net

"It's a Wonderful World" by Louis Armstrong; "These Are the Best Times of my Life" by….; One Singular Sensation" from Chorus Line; "My Way" by Frank Sinatra; "Fantasy" by Earth, Wind and Fire

Submitted by **Shari Roth**, Weston, Florida

"It's amazing what a positive impact great music has on me. These songs keep me focused on the positive side of life, personal as well as professional."

Shari is a Managing Partner with CAPITAL Idea— providing employee management training and sales training consulting to help organizations reach the goals that are important to them.

Learn more at: www.capital-idea.net and/or shari@capital-idea.net

GEORGIA:

"Edge of 17" by Stevie Nicks

Submitted by **Robin Martinelli**, Grayson, Georgia

"Even though the song is cool and upbeat and puts me in a positive mood, it is also all about working through challenges in your life, coming out on top and being proud of yourself."

Robin is a private investigator and President of Martinelli Investigations, Inc., a certified private investigations and process serving agency for civil and criminal cases.

Learn more at: www.martinelliinvestigations.com and/or gapprivateeye@bellsouth.net

MARYLAND:

"I Can See Clearly Now" by Johnny Nash

Submitted by **Eileen Nonemaker**, Eastern Shore of Maryland

"I chose this song because it represents a breakthrough. After many years of teaching, sales and sales management, for me this song speaks to those who have either been troubled, confused or just unguided and now "see" the answers and path that can take them forward. Coaching can be part of that process."

Eileen is a certified business coach and regional director for Paradigm Associates, LLC. She works with individuals and organizations to help them develop and implement success strategies.

Learn more at: www.paradigmassociates.us

"High Hopes" by Frank Sinatra

Submitted by **Amy E. Ryzenga**, Annapolis, Maryland

"This is a song that I sang with my family when I was growing up and we also sing it with my own family today. It is uplifting and fun to sing and keeps you thinking and moving forward in a positive direction."

Amy is a Principle at InternaSource, LLC, a private
practice that focuses on helping businesses and
individuals achieve success through management
consulting, leadership development, strategic
planning, and life and business coaching.

Learn more at: www.internasource.com

MASSACHUSETTS:

"If You're Going Through Hell" by Rodney Adkins

Submitted by **Anne La Perriere**, Haverhill, Massachusetts

"I listen to music every morning and it completely transforms
my state of mind. The words and the music to this song just
push out all the negativity and move me into a fresh new place."

"Settlin'" by Sugarland

Submitted by **Monique Sylvia**, Sutton, Massachusetts

"The song is about romance, but I apply it to everyday
life. 'Settlin' reminds me not to settle for just ordinary,
but to reach for what I want and for what I deserve."

Monique is the owner of Painted Treasures Located
in Sutton, MA, where she specializes in hand painted
glassware—"Gifts to Treasure for a Lifetime."

Learn more at: www.paintedtreasuresgifts.com
and/or mdsylvia@charter.net

"Drift Away" by Dobie Gray, "Lean on Me" by Bill Withers, "You've Got a Friend" by James Taylor, and "Wind Beneath my Wings" by Bette Midler.

Submitted by **Russ Sylvia**, Sutton, Massachusetts

"Each of these songs, in their own way, either relax me or

make me feel grateful for the friends and family that I have and to remember never take them for granted. Success and life is built on everyone being there for each other."

Russ is in Human Resources for a
Fortune 500 health care company.

MISSOURI:

"Here Comes the Sun" by The Beatles

Submitted by **Tom Schweizer**, Chesterfield, Missouri

"We all have days when things are not going right and we feel like we are under a cloud of doom. Yet, we find it in ourselves to work things out and feel a renewed optimism that things are good again."

Tom is a Not-For-Profit mentor, coach and
speaker—helping Not-For-Profits build success.

He is also a leadership coach for middle
school and high school students.

Learn more at: www.notforprofitsuccess.com
and/or tws@notforprofitsuccess.com

"Thank You for Being my Friend" by Andrew Gold, "It's My Job" by Jimmy Buffet, "One Day at a Time" by Joe Walsh

Submitted by **Wes Wingfield**, Kansas City, Missouri

"These songs all have related concepts—that that it's my job to be better than the rest, take the best from whatever the situation is and go on—and you don't have to go it alone."

Wes is a business coach and President, owner, founder
of Highest Ambition. Hope big a goal would you set if
you were assured of success? He works with his clients to
achieve improved results and a return on their investment.

Learn more at: www.highestAMBITION.com
and/or wes.wingfield@highestAMBITION.com

NEW HAMPSHIRE:

"I Am Woman" by Helen Reddy

Submitted by **Debby Hoffman Adair**,
Milford, New Hampshire

"My favorite line I use from a song comes from the
Helen Reddy song 'I Am Woman.' It reminds me to
be true to myself—that I am strong, have had unique
experiences, and don't have to pretend to be someone
I'm not. I use it when I need to go forward in something,
even if it is easier to stay still or step backward."

Debby is an award winning humorist, author, inspirational
speaker, radio host, and serial entrepreneur.

Learn more at: www.DebbyHoffman.com;
www.jigsawconsulting.org; www.PositiveWomen.com;
www.thisfield.com

"I Love You More Today than Yesterday" by Spiral Staircase

Submitted by **Pauline Lima**, Nashua, New Hampshire

"This is one of my favorites. I find the music and lyrics
very upbeat and positive, looking at the future..."

Pauline is a nurse.

NEW JERSEY:

"You're Only Human" (Second Wind) by Elton John

Submitted by **Celeste Kline**, New Jersey

Celeste is the Publisher of The Guilford County
Women's Journal, a bi-monthly resource
for the Women of Guilford County

Learn more at: gcwjournal@yahoo.com

NEW YORK:

"Suddenly I See" by K T Tunstall

Submitted by **Jean A. Oursler**, New York City, New York

"The words in this song make me feel strong and powerful.
It helps me to appreciate the beautiful person that I am when
I am not feeling as wonderful as I should. This song is in
the movie *The Devil Wears Prada* and when I hear it, I think
of Andy starting out on a new journey, how she grew and
what she achieved. I realize that each day I'm starting on a
new journey as well. This song says grow and achieve now
and that is what I try to achieve for myself every day."

Jean is owner of J.ALDEN Consulting Group and a
business coach helping organizations achieve dramatic
results by improving organizational operations and
processes in maximizing efficiency and profits.

Learn more at: www.jaldenco.com
and/or joursler@jaldenco.com

"I Can See Clearly Now" by Jimmy Cliff

Submitted by **Julie Walsh**, Brooklyn, New York

"I love that song—I remember singing that song with my sister
Adrienne when we were kids—while walking or running to
"get in shape" or whilst driving from NJ to Pittsburgh and
back—I associate it with good things because, when it was
on, we didn't think about anything else - we just turned it up
and just enjoyed ourselves and it helped dissipate whatever
the current anxieties happened to be—if only for 2 minutes!

It made me feel hopeful. Also it helped us to keep running!"

Julie is working at a video post-production company
in the Vault, and apprenticing there as well.

NORTH CAROLINA:

"Kvinnor Som Springer" by Frida

Submitted by **Virginia Adamson**, Madison, North Carolina

"This song helps me remember how strong women are!"

Virginia is a wife, mother, and working woman
who advocates for women and family issues.

Learn more at: virginia.adamson@yahoo.com

"Brick House" by The Commodores

Submitted by **Debbie Bergeron**, Greensboro, North Carolina

"This song puts me in a 'sexy mood' as I dance to it! It's been
a favorite of mine since my high school days in the 1970's!"

Debbie is a Domestic Diva that is a part-owner of Marshall
Art Gallery. She is also a mother and grandmother
(call me Nana Deb), a singer in a church choir and
in a community choral group, and a seamstress.

Learn more at: litldeb320@triad.rr.com

"Celebration" by Kool and the Gang

Submitted by **Alfred Bolton**, Greensboro, North Carolina

"Whenever I am low or in a funk, it is because I am not so
grateful for all the things both good and bad that happen
in my life. So I have a Daily Gratitude List, however small
or grand, that keeps me focused on the good and not the

negative. It can be a beautiful morning, a kind word for others, or sometimes just being alive. My central theme has and continues to be that life is a celebration and the choices I make determine the type of celebration."

Alfred has an international textile business
that has heavy dealings with China.

Learn more at: FabricsInternational@gmail.com

"Think of You" by Ledisi

Submitted by **Wendi Cash**, Burlington, North Carolina

"When you first listen, you might be mistaken that Ledisi is singing about her lover or child, but when you really listen, you discover that she is singing about the One we serve. It is a tribute to God - A love song to the One who loves us the most. It is so upbeat and the lyrics are so on point! I listen to this song when I am feeling the need to be uplifted or when I am in a great mood and want to celebrate it!

There is another song by Ledisi - "Alright" that I also
enjoy a lot. It reminds me that even though life throws
curve balls and setbacks, it is not over. There are still
other things to celebrate and be happy about. Don't
sweat the small stuff...it's going to be all right!

Wendi is an event and travel planner.

Learn more at: www.wceventsllc.com
and/or wc_events@yahoo.com

"How Great Thou Art" hymn sung by many artists and "My Redeemer Lives" by Mandella

Submitted by **Jane Creech**, Greensboro, North Carolina

"I know that God is in control of every second of every day and only by His grace, a free gift, are we given each breath. He loved us first and His thoughts of us outnumber the grains on His earth. God is my Comforter and Redeemer every day — so I sing 'How Great thou Art.'"

Jane is the owner of Response Link of the Triad, a personal medical alert system, enhancing your safety and insuring your independence.

Learn more at: www.responselink.com and/or JaneCreech@responselink.com

"Don't Worry, Be Happy" by Bobby McFerrin

Submitted by **Erinn Diaz**, Winston-Salem, North Carolina

"Over the years, I have learned over and over again that everything happens for a reason. If there's ever a road block on my path to life, I love to listen to this song to remind myself that nothing is really worth worrying over in life!"

Erinn Diaz is the President of First in Flight Entertainment in North Carolina and the author of *Help! I'm On My Own and Don't Know Where To Start! An Essential Guide to Living on your Own* by Erinn Dearth.

Learn more at: www.FirstInFlightEntertainment.com

"Somewhere Over the Rainbow" sung by Israel Kamakawiwo'Ole

Submitted by **Nelson Diaz**, Winston-Salem, North Carolina

"I chose this song...because there IS a treasure under a rainbow for those that look beyond the rain. Dream your dreams, stop, think and make a 5 year plan/goal. Divide that into 5 equal parts/goals - one per year. Then into month goals, week goals and daily goals where the smaller goals complete the next level ones. Now you have a daily routine that when you follow it will lead you to your dreams in 5 years. That's how laid back it is to reach your dreams, so dream big because when you aim for that rainbow you'll see what a wonderful world there is inside of it."

Nelson is an Entrepreneur who loves to mentor, has been all

over the world and has seen many rainbows of all kinds.

Learn more at: www.christmasornamentsandwoodcraft.com
and/or solidinvestment@hotmail.com

"Count Your Blessings" by Diana Krall

Submitted by **Greer Ducker**, Greensboro, North Carolina

"This song reminds me of the achievements I have
made over my lifetime and that there is always
someone else who is experiencing a lot tougher
issues than my petty problem of the day."

Greer is a financial advisor with Edward Jones Investments.

Learn more a: www.edwardjones.com and/or
Greer.Ducker@edwardjones.com

"Change the World" by Debbie Zepick

Submitted by **Kristen Eckstein**,
High Point, North Carolina

"This is one of my favorite songs of all time. I've sung
it at church and absolutely love the message it conveys.
Its Celtic theme and music is relaxing, yet energetic, and
its message is one each of us holds somewhere deep
inside. When I listen to it, my confidence increases and
I get excited about my God-given mission in life to not
be afraid to change the world before I'm gone."

Kristen is the Executive Producer of Imagine! Studios.

Learn more at: www.ultimatebookcoach.com
and/or www.artsimagine.com

"Lighthouse of Hope" by Abby Sutton, "You Lift Me Up" by Josh Grobin, and "I'm so Excited" by The Pointer Sisters

Submitted by **"Simply" Sue Falcone**,
Greensboro, North Carolina

"I love songs that reach down into your soul and inspire you to do great things. I co-wrote 'Lighthouse of Hope' with Abby Sutton, which was inspired by my book. The songs can be hymn-like or just fun!"

"Simply" Sue is a Speaker Who Writes - and a Motivational & Inspirational Speaker, Teacher, & Author

Learn more at: www.simplysuespeaks.com and/or simplysue@att.net

"Carolina On My Mind" by James Taylor; "Unforgettable" by Nat King Cole; "Ain't No Mountain High Enough" by Diana Ross

Submitted by **Lisa Freeman**, High Point, North Carolina

"I have enjoyed the various transitions in my career paths and with each one have learned more about myself and how each of us can make a difference one person at time. These songs always bring me back to the love of my life, my family and the possibilities of what we can do."

Lisa's is enjoying building her business as a Shaklee Director, "Where we provide a healthier life for everyone and a better life for anyone." Tm

Learn more at: www.freeman-associates.myshaklee.com and/or lfreeman@triad.rr.com

"Yahweh" by U2

Submitted by **Greg Giordano**, High Point, North Carolina

"It is a reminder to me of what is most important in life."

Greg is an affiliate for Send Out Cards, which helps businesses with customer appreciation and retention. Try it for free!

Learn more at: www.SendOutCards.com/22469 and/or gsgiordano@gmail.com

"The Climb" by Miley Cyrus

Submitted by **C.E. Hacker**, Greensboro/
Winston-Salem, North Carolina

"It reminds that the journey is what is important.
The hard parts are when we grow."

C.E. is the owner of C.E. Hacker Consulting—a
professional training and coaching industry;
freelance writing, speech/presentation
coaching, computer support/training.

Learn more at: www.cehackerconsulting.com and/or
unleashyourpotential@cehackerconsulting.com

"It's the God in Me" by Mary Mary

Submitted by **Je T'aime**, The Triangle, North Carolina

"This song makes me remember that there is something inside
each of us that is special, and the more we search for it by
praying and being thankful, the better person we will be."

JeT'aime is an actress, a dancer, a plus model,
an emcee/host, a voice over talent, spoken
word artist, and motivational speaker.

Learn more at: www.jetaime4u.com
and/or jetaime@jetaime4u.com

"Three Little Birds" by Bob Marley

Submitted by **Ronda Katzman**, Charlotte, North Carolina

"I would say that there are only a few songs that inspire
a smile on my face during troubled times. This song is a
reminder to me of the simple things in life that offer joy,
even when we do not go seeking it. We need to remember
truly our joy *can* be found in the simple things."

Ronda is a Business Performance Consultant with Spectrum

Consulting Group, LLC. She is a business consultant to small businesses. Many of them are hurting, struggling, and feeling desperate for solutions to their business woes. Here again, their solution can often be found in the little things.

Learn more at: rspectrum09@yahoo.com

"Imagine" by John Lennon and "The Man in the Mirror" by Michael Jackson

Submitted by **Joe Kelly**, Greensboro, North Carolina

"Wouldn't it be nice if this imagination would come true? Wouldn't it be nice if we were happy with ourselves and proud of who we were and what we did? Perhaps there would be peace, beginning with each of us, that would allow everyone to live peacefully with each other."

Joe is the owner of Awards of Excellence - trophies, plaques, certificates, awards, acrylic engraving, bronze castings, buttons, desk name plates

Learn more at: www.awardsofexcellence.com and/or Trophy789@aol.com

"Jumping Jack Flash" by The Rolling Stones

Submitted by **Skip Lovette**, Greensboro, North Carolina

"It's a gas!"

Skip is the owner of Skip Lovett, CPA — business, tax, and financial services

Learn more at: www.skiplovettecpa.com

"Wind Beneath My Wings" by Bette Midler or Queen Latifa and

"You Take My Breath Away" the theme song from Top Gun

Submitted by **Andree Martin**, Greensboro, North Carolina

"The first song is soothing and reminds me what one individual can do in a big way and quietly. It reminds me of the light and support our God has for us when we allow it. I love to inspire and it inspires me.

The second song just gets my energy levels up and motivates me to let my hair down and go for it!"

Andree is a LPGA Class A professional, a nationally recognized Top 50 Teacher and Expert. She is also a golf instruction specialist, a writer, and a speaker. She heads up golf instruction at Promontory in Park City, Utah in the summer and teaches at Carolina Golf in Greensboro, NC in the winter.

Learn more at: www.andregolf.com and/or andree@andreegolf.com

"Because You Loved Me" by Celine Dion

Submitted by **Jan McDiarmid**, Greensboro, North Carolina

"I decided on this song as a tribute to my husband, Stuart, for believing in me with my business and my dreams for success."

Jan is the owner of Digital Introductions—developing and producing video business cards, video presentations, personalized flashdrives, video e-mail, video real estate tours, and video testimonials.

Learn more at: www.digitalintros.com and/or digitalintroductions@gmail.com

"I Will Survive" by Gloria Gaynor

Submitted by **Mary G. Mora**, Winston-Salem, North Carolina

"No matter what the circumstances—keep a positive attitude!"

Mary G. is a talent connector and the owner of MGM Speakers Bureau. Meeting your needs—Helping you reach your goals! MGM Speakers Bureau provides motivational keynote speakers, customized training, and business coaches from coast to coast.

Learn more at: http://mgmspeakersbureau.com
and/or maryg@mgmspeakersbureau.com

"Crocodile Rock" by Elton John, "Don't Stop" by Fleetwood Mac, "Little Red Corvette" by Prince, "I'm Yours" by Jason Mraz' "What a Wonderful World" by Nat King Cole.

Submitted by **Renea Myers**, Greensboro, North Carolina

"The music to these songs just gets me going and singing and makes me laugh. I also like many of the songs that my little boy likes and we enjoy singing them together."

Renea Myers is the owner of Renea Myers Marketing—
offering complete outsourced marketing departments
for companies that so not have one. We also work with
companies on short-terms projects and events.

Learn more at: www.rmyersmarketing.com
and/or renea@rmyersmarketing.com

"Hail to the King" by Shannon Wexelberg

Submitted by **Mary Needham**, Greensboro, North Carolina

"This song takes the focus off of me and puts it on God, where it should be and puts me in a better place. When we focus on ourselves too much, life can be distorted. It's like changing your life from looking through a prism to a clear glass and truly being able to see what God has for you."

Mary is the owner of Greater Expectations
Catering and Meals To Go—a full service catering
kitchen—your secret weapon for bringing the
tastiest morsels to your home or event.

Learn more at: www.GreaterExpectationsCatering.com
and/or mary@GreaterExpectationsCatering.com

"Gonna Make You Sweat" by C&C Music Factory and "Come Out and Play, Keep 'em Separated" by Offspring

Submitted by **Kay Mowery-Seufer**,
Kernersville, North Carolina

"Music is a large part of my life. Not only does it express how I feel, it is a useful tool to change your mood as well. Both songs listed are part of my workout playlist. They carry their own energy which is a powerful tool when getting to the next level or sometimes just getting to the end of the workout. Enjoy."

Kay is an accountant with Barbara H.
Fulp & Company, PLLC.

Learn more at: www.barbarafulpcpa.com

"Stray Cat Strut" by Stray Cats

Submitted by **Cheri Osterholt**, Greensboro, North Carolina

"This song puts a smile on my face. It reminds me of my childhood and riding in the back of my parents' truck in the country."

Cheri is a stylist, a color specialist, and the owner of Salon Medusa.

Look us up on Facebook: Salon Medusa

"My Time" by Kindred the Family Soul

Submitted by **Nishaka Proctor**, Greensboro, North Carolina

"I love this song because it tells my story. It talks about going through tough times, but overcoming it. It talks about hope and being ready because it's my time to achieve and do anything I believe and put my heart and mind to doing. It is about having faith, taking action, being rich in love, rich in peace, and being rich in hope."

Nishaka is an events coordinator offering first-class planning for extraordinary events.

Learn more at: www.EventsWithExcellence.com
and/or NProctor@EventsWithExcellence.com

"The Theme from Love Boat"

Submitted by **Tom Pullara**, Greensboro, North Carolina

"The song is short, sweet, and lively. I can picture myself relaxing and unwinding on a cruise ship or on a tropical island, escaping the routine of everyday life. When I return, I'm refreshed and ready for the new challenges ahead of me."

Tom is a travel agent with Cruise One. Let us help you with your next cruise or vacation…because…Yes! We know fun!!!

Learn more at: www.cruiseone.com/kallred

www.membercruises.com/Hear/Applause
and/or tom@medform.com

"You Raise Me Up" by Josh Grobin

Submitted by **Gina Reese**, **Karen Hamston** and
Nikki Harris, Greensboro, North Carolina

"Even faced with the biggest struggles, we can lift ourselves up, either alone or with the help of others. We can also be rewarded by helping people become better in society. At A.C.T Fitness, we help people develop the best exercise and health routines that will help them overcome their obstacles."

Gina, Karen, and Nikki are personal fitness trainers at A.C.T Fitness in Greensboro, NC. — An Alternative to Crowded Gyms. They work with beginners, people who haven't exercised in years, those who need to address medical issues or injuries and professional athletes. Se Habla Español.

Learn more at: www.actbydeese.com

"With a Little Help from my Friends" by The Beatles

Submitted by **Lorrie Z. Roth**, Julian, North Carolina

"I have good friends and I try to be a good friend. It's in the cultivating of good friendships that makes this journey we call life the most wonderful experience we can ever have! My life is positively affected by so many of the great friendships I've been lucky enough to plant and grow. Truly no one has to go it alone, and with a good friend at your side you always have someone to row with whenever you are too tired to lift the oar."

Lorrie is the Coordinator with the Piedmont Triad
Community Resource Connection for Aging & Disabilities.

Learn more at: lroth@co.guilford.nc.us

"Take a Giant Step" by The Monkees

Submitted by **Pat Sledge**, Winston-Salem, North Carolina

I've been a big fan of this song since I'd first heard it as a teen. It's always stayed with me. The message of the song is: The past is the past. Remember what you've learned and forge ahead. Be thankful for the wonders in your life."

Pat sells promotional products needs and is
a representative for Ad Pro Solutions.

Learn more at: http://www.distributorcentral.com/websites/
AdProSolutionsdivisionofClassicBusinessSystemsInc and
/or http://www.LogomarkPortfolio.com/classic_adpro

"I've Got A Feeling" by The Black Eyed Peas

Submitted by **Ann Smith**, Greensboro, North Carolina

"My current favorite is this particular song. I like to listen to it before I go out to my Silpada parties. It is fun and upbeat—just like our parties are! I love helping women get free jewelry." Ann is a Silpada Designs Representative and when she goes to work— she ends up at a party!

Learn more at: www.mysilpada.com/ann.smith

"Broken Road" by Rascal Flats

Submitted by **Megan Snipes**, Kernersville, North Carolina

"This song has great memories attached to it. It was at a Rascal Flats concert about 5 years ago when Greg and I first realized that we loved each other. The rest, as they say, is history…"

Megan is a stylist and color specialist at Salon Medusa.

Become a fan of Salon Medusa on Facebook and/or contact her at: meganfree03@yahoo.com

"You Send Me" by Sam Cooke

Submitted by **Lauren Stagner**, Greensboro, North Carolina

"This is the song my husband and I danced to at our wedding. It reminds me of when we met and happy times we have together."

Lauren is a wedding planner, interior designer, dancer, and "Jill of all trades."

Learn more at: www.felicitycreative.com and /or lauren@felicitycreative.com

"Stand By Me" from You Tube

Submitted by **Mike Stipanov**, Greensboro, North Carolina

"Watch this video 'Stand By Me' from You Tube. It's a little over 5 minutes long and needs to be watched until the end.

Go to www.playingforchange.com and you will see how this video was done and what the producer's mission is—peace around the world through the link and common thread of music. Listen to the words and then visit the website. Everyone needs someone in times of change, development, crisis, growth, etc. In choosing success someone needs to stand by that person as a friend, mentor, teacher, etc."

Mike is a financial advisor with Edward Jones Investments.

Learn more at: www.edwardjones.com
and/or mikestipanov@yahoo.com

"Circle" by Harry Chapin

Submitted by **Charlotte Stoll**, Greensboro, North Carolina

"When I think of a song that always makes me feel centered, it is 'Circle'. When our girls were growing up, we would be in the car or at home, put in the "cassette tape" and loudly sing along, their friends included. The girls remember still, as a matter of fact, one of our daughters had it played at her wedding for the father/daughter dance. Life is indeed a circle."

Charlotte is a long term care planner/consultant.

Learn more at: www.seniorcareconcepts.com
and/or cares05@triad.rr.com

"Paradise" by John Prine

Submitted by **Don Summerford** Winston-Salem, North Carolina

"This song speaks to the innocence of a young boy who loved visiting his grandparents, appreciated God's glorious creations, and was saddened to see it disappear quickly due to the progress of man."

Don is the Director of New Business Development for The Lattitude Group.

Learn more at: www.lattitudegroup.com
and/or don@tlgrp.com

"We are the Champions of the World" by Queen

Submitted by **Hank Williamson**,
Greensboro, North Carolina

The music is upbeat and the lyrics speak of persevering...
'we'll keep on fighting til the end, cause...' When the lyrics run
through your mind, you are inspired to meet the challenges
of the day and seize the opportunities. Your thoughts go
beyond self-reflection, because the song speaks of a collective
'we'. It's together—the team, the co-workers, the family—
together we are strong and we become champions."

Hank is the owner of the Maids Home Services,
where "nobody out cleans the maids."

Learn more at: www.maids.com and/or
maidshpgnc@bellsouth.com

PENNSYLVANIA:

"Respect" by Aretha Franklin and "Pachalbel Cannon in D Major" by Johann Pachalbel

Submitted by Nancy Stauffer, Lancaster, Pennsylvania

"'Respect' gets me up off my butt and moving—
even to cleaning the house—a job I hate!

'Patchalbel' gets me into deep but positive thoughts."

Nancy is President of Maximum Potential
Corporation International.

Learn more at: www.maximumpotentialcorp.com